LEADING THE UNKNOWN

Nuri Demirci López

DEDICATION

This book is dedicated to my beloved family, to my wife Monique, whose endless support and love have been my anchor, and to my sons, Alex and Mert, who have always stood by me, no matter the circumstances. Their presence and belief in me have been my constant source of strength and inspiration.

I extend a special dedication to the many leaders and colleagues who have journeyed with me, sculpting my professional path and personal growth. Their influence has been immeasurable, shaping me into the individual I am today.

Lastly, to the myriad of gig workers, I have had the privilege of working alongside: you have been my teachers in ways more profound than words can express. The knowledge and experiences you shared with me have been invaluable, and I am eternally grateful for this.

PROLOGUE

As I begin the process of writing my first book, I am filled with a mix of uncertainty and excitement. This book is more than just a reflection of my extensive experience; it is a step into the new territory of authorship. My focus is on the challenges and opportunities of leading a globally dispersed organization. This includes managing a team I have never met in person, each member bringing their own experience, cultural background, and professional insight. This book primarily addresses leadership in the remote or gig-freelance ecosystem, but the insights it offers are universally applicable to leadership in a globally connected world. It underscores the idea that effective leadership continually evolves, embracing diversity and adapting to the shifting landscape of the global workforce.

At first glance, you might believe that guiding the uncharted is a task already performed by leaders in different domains, including military, government, business, or organizations. Within these domains, we can find numerous instances of both successes and failures in leadership. A significant amount of literature exists on the analysis of great leaders. On the pages of *Hind Swaraj*, a dialogue between the reader and the editor unfolds, portraying Gandhi's vision for an India free from colonial rule, written during his voyage from London to South Africa in 1909. As the editor, Gandhi counters the reader's conventional arguments for independence with profound insights into self-rule, or *swaraj*. This text, deemed seditious and banned by the British in 1910, captures Gandhi's transformative ideology, which later culminated in the nonviolent resistance movement that led to India's independence. Gandhi's leadership here is marked by his revolutionary concept of nonviolent action and civil disobedience, which inspired not just a nation but the entire world. This is excellent leadership with care and wisdom, but we will not go down that path. Our caring leadership concept will focus on organizations and corporations.

Our case is quite unique, focusing on the workplace environment, which often includes gig and freelancing scenarios, primarily in a remote setting. However, the insights in this book are not limited to these types of workers alone. The content is geared towards the business and corporate world, particularly addressing the needs of remote teams. A significant portion of the book relates to managing and leading remote teams of gig workers and freelancers, nevertheless it is not limited to them. The experiences and practices discussed will provide guidance on how to effectively lead individuals in the business world, impact their lives positively, and align them with a common business goal.

I draw inspiration from a wealth of extraordinary books and authors. Take, for instance, Simon Sinek's *Leaders Eat Last: Why Some Teams Pull Together and Others Don't*. In this work, Sinek delves into the concept of effective leadership, emphasizing the creation of a trust-filled and cooperative environment achieved when leaders prioritize their team's needs over their own interests.

Likewise, Brené Brown's book, *The Gifts Of Imperfection*, serves as another wellspring of inspiration. Brown's work guides readers on the path to embracing their imperfections and living a wholehearted life. Her wisdom encourages the practice of self-love, self-compassion, and the formation of genuine connections with others, all while liberating oneself from societal pressures and expectations.

In my book, I aim to take the lofty principles of great leadership and ground them in the realities of today's work environment. The domains of gig, freelance, and remote work are not just flourishing; they are becoming the preferred mode of operation in both small-scale ventures and large corporations. This shift puts a spotlight on remote workers, especially those in the freelancer and gig economy, who are inherently operating from afar. My goal is to address certain gaps and overlooked aspects in leaderships I have encountered and appreciated. This book is designed to aid corporations that are expanding their remote and gig workforce. It is about choosing leaders who are not just adept at meeting business objectives but are also capable of fostering a robust community of gig and freelance workers united in their pursuit of a common goal. Through this, I seek to create a blueprint for leadership that resonates with the unique demands and opportunities of managing a distributed workforce, ensuring that unity and purpose remain at the heart of the corporate ethos, regardless of physical location.

The concept of leadership is a fascinating study in contrasts between theory and practice. This topic has captivated minds and spurred endless discussions, particularly in the United States, where the abundance of literature on this subject is nothing short of staggering. There are over 150,000 books dedicated to the exploration of various facets of leadership, not to mention the countless articles written on the topic. This extensive ocean of content includes everything from inspiring tales of exceptional leaders to practical tips on how to evolve into a leadership role.

There is also a fair share of discourse on ineffective leadership, offering insights into avoiding such pitfalls.

Yet, amidst this vast expanse of guidance and anecdotes, my book presents a somewhat different perspective: leaders are not so much made as they are born. This assertion might seem controversial in the face of the extensive literature suggesting otherwise, but it is a stance I firmly believe in. This book does not dismiss the value of learning and growth; it acknowledges that one's leadership style can and should be refined over time. However, it suggests that the essence of a leader, the innate ability to inspire, guide, and influence, is something ingrained, and an intrinsic part of one's character.

This book explores this idea, delving into what sets naturally born leaders apart and how these innate qualities manifest in different environments and situations. It also recognizes the journey of personal development, acknowledging that while the seeds of leadership may be inherent, their nurturing, cultivation, and growth are equally important. It is about understanding the blend of inborn traits and learned skills that come together to shape a leader.

Furthermore, the book aims to bridge the gap between the romanticized version of leadership often portrayed in literature and the pragmatic realities of leading in diverse and challenging environments. In doing so, it provides a fresh perspective on what it means to be a leader, challenging readers to reflect on their own leadership potential and how it aligns with the conventional wisdom in this field. This book is a collection of practices I have learned, primarily through a series of experiences and, more significantly, through numerous failures. It is designed as a resource for natural-born leaders, offering them a wealth of insights and strategies that I have gleaned from my own journey. The emphasis here is on the invaluable lessons that come from stumbling and falling, as these moments often provide the richest learning opportunities.

Each practice detailed in the book reflects a real-world scenario, a challenge faced, or a hurdle overcome. I believe that even those inherently gifted in leadership can greatly benefit from understanding and applying these lessons. The book is more than just a guide; it is a compilation of lived experiences, offering a unique perspective that blends theoretical leadership concepts with practical, hard-earned wisdom. The book you will read is a journey into the heart of leadership, a venture into understanding its innate qualities, and a guide to nurturing and honing these abilities. It is a story that intertwines the inherent and the acquired aspects of leadership, offering a nuanced view that respects the complexity and depth of what it truly means to lead.

My conviction is that the core of true leadership is beyond the reach of individuals who lack the foundational attributes, no matter their dedication or scholarly endeavors. For instance, consider the innate strategic genius of Hannibal Barca in ancient times. Despite the military norms and tactics of his era, he led with an instinctual grasp of warfare that no amount of study could solely bestow. In a more modern context, take Steve Jobs, whose visionary foresight and charismatic leadership reshaped the tech industry. His ability to intuitively understand market desires and innovate accordingly was not just the product of his reading or formal education but a natural leadership acumen. These historical figures exemplify that while education can refine and enhance leadership, it cannot implant the natural intuition and innate qualities that constitute the bedrock of a natural leader. In the business ecosystem, the absence of innate leadership qualities can lead to notable failures.

Over the past six years, my professional journey has been profoundly influenced by the changing landscape of the workplace, the transformation in the way work is executed, and the evolving methods of its delivery. This period has been marked by significant shifts in workplace dynamics, signaling new approaches and methodologies that have reshaped my experience and growth in the field. Tasked with the challenge of building a global, fully remote gig-freelancing workforce for various business purposes, I dove headfirst into a world where each day brought new lessons about this flourishing domain. Before the pandemic, the gig economy was already a thriving ecosystem, yet it was marked by certain deficiencies. Many gig workers lacked a sense of identity. There was a notable absence of community, collaboration, social good, knowledge sharing, and mentoring. These observations struck a chord with me, fueling my belief in a future where work is predominantly remote and gig-based.

This belief became my driving force, presenting a unique opportunity to not only uphold the fundamental principles of gig work but also to reimagine and shape how a gig community could be developed, nurtured, and led with purpose and identity. The journey was not without its challenges. Navigating through a maze of legal, tools, and process constraints required tenacity and innovation. Yet, overcoming these hurdles led to the creation of a model that stands as evidence of what the future of work could look like, a model of democratized work that can be easily adapted by corporations preparing for future work dynamics.

The insights and experiences gained from this journey form the core of my book. It is a narrative not just of my learnings but also of the invaluable lessons learned from interactions with gig workers, collaborations with gig platforms, and, importantly, from my missteps. This book is an exploration of the stages and transformations I experienced in shaping a new way of work. It is a story of resilience, innovation, and the relentless pursuit of a vision where the gig economy is not just a fringe element of the labor market but a central, vibrant, and equitable part of the future of work. This journey, filled with trials, triumphs, and transformations, offers insights and strategies for organizations and individuals alike, preparing them for a future where work is not confined by physical boundaries but is liberated by technology, innovation, and a shared sense of purpose and community.

In this book, we will delve into the art of communication that transcends barriers, crafting visions that act as a siren call to unity, and fostering environments where differences are not just tolerated but celebrated as keystones of strength and innovation. We will explore the subtle alchemy of turning a group of disparate individuals into a cohesive and dynamic force capable of achieving more together than they ever could apart.

In today's complex and often challenging business environment, this book serves as a practical guide and a commitment to the idea that it is possible to unite diverse individuals toward a common goal with empathy, understanding, and strategic foresight. We embark on an exploration of modern leadership, aiming to understand how to effectively utilize the diverse potential of our global workforce to achieve not only success but also meaningful impact.

The following chapters delve into these critical questions, offering a journey into the core of global leadership challenges. This book combines practical experience with research to provide insights and strategies for navigating these complex times. My goal is to equip readers with a set of tools and perspectives drawn from both real-world experience and academic study to effectively lead in today's dynamic business landscape.

As we go through this book, I hope that the stories and lessons shared will provide clear guidance on how to lead effectively and empathetically. I aim to inspire readers, encouraging current and aspiring leaders to confidently adopt and implement the concepts and ideas presented. This book is intended to be a source of motivation, helping leaders tackle the complexities of modern leadership with confidence and insight.

Note to the reader: In the pages of this book, I will intentionally employ the terms "manager" and "leader" with distinct purpose, carefully choosing each to highlight their unique connotations and roles. Their usage is deliberate, underscoring the nuanced differences between these two pivotal roles rather than using them interchangeably.

INTRODUCTION

Remote work, often perceived as a pandemic-driven necessity, was gaining traction well before 2020, propelled by a confluence of technological, demographic, and economic factors. Technologically, the landscape preceding the pandemic was ready for remote work. The widespread availability of high-speed internet, like the railways during the Industrial Revolution, connected remote corners of the world, facilitating seamless communication. This was further augmented by the proliferation of cloud computing and collaboration tools. A 2019 report by Owl Labs[1] revealed that 52% of workers globally worked remotely at least once a week, illustrating a significant shift towards remote work environments before the pandemic.

Demographically, the workforce was undergoing a significant transition. Millennials and Gen Z, who entered the workforce with a different set of priorities compared to previous generations, were like the fresh winds that changed the course of a sailboat. They sought flexibility, work-life balance, and autonomy, aspects that remote work offered. A survey by Buffer[2] in 2019 found that 99% of respondents wanted to work remotely at least part-time for the rest of their careers, indicating a clear preference for this way of work even before it became a necessity.

Economically, businesses were beginning to recognize the benefits of remote work, comparable to the way industries in the past realized the efficiency of assembly lines. Remote work promised reduced overhead costs, access to a broader talent pool, and potentially higher productivity. A survey conducted by FlexJobs[3] in 2019 found that 80% of companies offered some form of remote work option, showcasing an organizational shift towards this model before the pandemic hit the world. The analogy of climate change can be aptly applied here: just as climate change was a gradual process that went largely unnoticed until it reached a critical point, the shift towards remote work was a slowly developing trend that only became overwhelmingly apparent during the COVID-19 pandemic.

The adoption of remote work before the pandemic can be compared to the initial stages of a technological revolution. It was a gradual but undeniable shift, driven by a combination of technological advancements, changing workforce demographics, and economic incentives. In this scenario, the pandemic acted not as the initiator but as an accelerator, much like how a catalyst in a chemical reaction speeds up a process already underway. This pre-pandemic momentum towards remote work proves the evolving nature of work in the 21st century, shaped by a confluence of diverse but interconnected factors.

The pre-COVID-19 growth of the gig and freelancing sector is a narrative of gradual yet significant change, like the steady rise of a tide rather than a sudden wave. This shift, deeply rooted in the evolving nature of work and technology, was already reshaping the workforce landscape before the pandemic acted as a catalyst. To understand this trend, we can look at the gig economy's market value, a clear indicator of its health and trajectory. In 2019, the gig economy was valued at approximately 248.3 billion US$, according to a study conducted by Mastercard[4]. This substantial figure, comparable to the GDP of entire nations, highlights the sector's already strong presence and influence in the global economy. Further evidence of this growth can be seen in the increasing financial success of freelancers. By 2021, 44% of freelancers reported higher earnings from their gig work than from traditional employment, a notable increase from 32% in 2019. This increase is like a small plant growing into a big tree, with more people getting steady jobs in freelancing every year. Another critical measure of the gig sector's pre-pandemic strength is its economic contribution. In 2020, U.S. freelancers alone contributed a staggering 1.21 trillion US$ to the economy[5]. This contribution is not just a number; it is proof of the gig sector's role as a vital artery in the national economy, pumping financial lifeblood and supporting countless families.

The role of technology platforms in facilitating this growth cannot be overlooked. These platforms have acted like bridges, connecting a vast and diverse array of freelancers with global opportunities. By 2019, the infrastructure supporting the gig economy was already robust, enabling a seamless transition to an even greater reliance on remote and freelance work during the pandemic. The gig and freelancing wave was already gathering strength before the pandemic provided the wind to push it further ashore. This pre-existing momentum underscores the sector's resilience and its crucial role in the modern workforce. In this context, the pandemic served not as the creator of this trend but as a powerful amplifier, highlighting the adaptability and economic importance of gig and freelance work in a rapidly evolving world.

In recent years, the work landscape has undergone a profound transformation, a change I have had the privilege to witness and contribute to, both before and during the COVID-19 pandemic and now as we navigate its aftermath. The shift from traditional, office-based work to remote, gig, and freelance models has been nothing short of revolutionary. Initially, many organizations, steeped in conventional work practices, were hesitant to embrace remote work. However, the pandemic served as a catalyst, compelling even the most conservative companies to reconsider and progressively adopt remote work models. This trend has persisted beyond the pandemic, with many companies offering flexible, partially remote work options. During the COVID-19 pandemic, remote work proved to be not only feasible but also beneficial for many companies and employees. This shift was driven by necessity, showcasing the potential for more flexible work arrangements.

The transition to remote work during the pandemic was successful, even though management teams were initially unprepared. Tools like Microsoft Teams, Zoom, and Slack played a crucial role in bridging the physical gap between remote workers. A study by PwC[6] in January 2021 supported this success, revealing that 83% of employers found the shift to remote work beneficial for their company. However, as the world started recovering from the pandemic, some companies began reverting to traditional office settings despite having experienced the advantages of remote work.

Despite these positive outcomes, some companies are still hesitant to fully commit to remote work. This hesitance may be due to concerns about maintaining productivity, preserving corporate culture, or an inherent resistance to change. However, this approach overlooks the benefits observed during the pandemic, such as increased productivity, secure remote systems access, reduced operational costs, and access to a broader talent pool. For instance, Global Workplace Analytics[7] reported that a typical employer can save around 11,000 US$ per half-time telecommuter annually. Additionally, remote work offers environmental benefits by reducing the need for commuting, which adds to the carbon footprint's positive impact.

Despite its demonstrated advantages, the reluctance of some companies to fully embrace remote work reflects a cautious approach to adopting new work models. This situation presents a complex scenario where the future of work is still being shaped and influenced by both innovative practices and traditional work structures. As the workplace continues to evolve in the post-pandemic era, it remains to be seen how these contrasting perspectives will ultimately shape the way we work.

The future of work is inevitably steering towards remote and flexible models, and companies that fail to recognize this trend risk falling behind in an increasingly competitive marketplace. The pandemic has irreversibly shifted the landscape, demonstrating to employees across various industries the tangible benefits of remote work. These benefits are not just limited to personal convenience but extend to increased productivity, better work-life balance, and overall job satisfaction. Employees have tasted the freedom and flexibility that remote work offers and many are unwilling to revert to the rigid structures of traditional office environments.

There is an urgent need for companies to adapt to this changing paradigm. The risk of not doing so is substantial. The talented workforce, now more aware of the possibilities and benefits of remote work, is likely to gravitate toward employers who offer these options. This shift in employee preference is not merely a trend but a fundamental change in the workforce's expectations. Companies that cling to outdated work models risk losing their best employees to more progressive competitors. Even if it means accepting slightly lower salaries, many workers are now prioritizing flexibility and the quality of their work environment over traditional compensation packages.

This urgency is not just about retaining talent but also about attracting new talent. The next generation of workers, having witnessed the flexibility and effectiveness of remote work, will increasingly seek employers who offer such arrangements. Companies that are slow to adapt will find themselves at a significant disadvantage, struggling to attract the innovative and adaptable talent necessary to thrive in a rapidly evolving business landscape.

My message to companies is clear: the future of work is flexible, and remote work is a key component of this future. Ignoring this shift is not just a missed opportunity but a strategic misstep that could have long-lasting repercussions. The time to act is now; companies must embrace remote work and the flexibility it offers or risk being left behind in a world where adaptability, innovation, and employee well-being are paramount.

While remote work will dominate sooner than many think, the flourishing gig economy is no longer a novel trend. It has become a significant part of the global workforce, signaling an urgent call for companies to embrace this model regardless of their size. The article "What will the gig economy look like in 2023[8]" highlights the dramatic expansion of the gig economy, which is anticipated to attain a global value of 443 to 455 billion US$ by 2023. This remarkable growth signifies a profound transformation in employment trends and habits. This growth trajectory is not just a mere spike; it represents a fundamental change in how work is viewed, undertaken, and valued. Companies must recognize the urgency of this transition. The gig economy's appeal lies not just in its flexibility for workers but also in its myriad benefits for employers. From 2021 to 2028, the gig economy is expected to grow from 355 billion US$ to an astonishing 873 billion US$, according to the article "Gig Economy Trends 2023[9]", indicating an irreversible trend towards freelance and contract work. This evolution is driven by the rapid change in the types of talent companies need. Traditional employment models are increasingly inadequate in meeting these fast-evolving demands. With their diverse skill sets and ability to pivot quickly, Gig workers offer a solution to this challenge.

Moreover, the inclination of people towards gig work is rising. McKinsey's 2022 American Opportunity Survey[10] revealed that 36% of employed respondents were involved in the gig economy, a significant increase from 27% in 2016. This shift in worker preferences is a clear indicator to companies: the workforce is ready and willing to engage in more flexible, gig-based roles. By not adapting to this trend, companies risk missing out on top talent who prefer the flexibility and autonomy that gig work offers.

The message is evident and pressing: corporations must adjust to the gig economy or face the possibility of falling behind. This adaptation is not just about accessing a wider talent pool but about staying relevant in a rapidly changing business environment. With the gig economy's projected value reaching 455 billion US$ in 2023, up 53% from 2020, businesses need to recognize the economic and strategic imperative of embracing this model. The future of work is shifting towards gig and freelance opportunities, and companies that are quick to adapt to this change will be the ones to thrive in the evolving marketplace.

The swift expansion of the gig and freelance economy is progressing at a rate that surpasses the capacity of numerous governments to implement effective regulations and provide benefits for these workers. This sector, characterized by temporary, flexible jobs, is growing faster than traditional employment models. As a result, many governments are struggling to adapt their labor laws and social security systems to protect the rights and welfare of gig workers. This disconnect poses significant challenges, not just for the workers themselves but also for the broader economic and social systems. Traditional employment laws and benefits systems were designed in an era where full-time, permanent jobs were the norm, and they have not yet fully adapted to the realities of modern, flexible work arrangements. At the heart of the issue is the classification of gig and freelance workers. In many jurisdictions, these workers are often considered independent contractors, which excludes them from many of the protections and benefits afforded to full-time employees. This includes access to healthcare, unemployment benefits, workers' compensation, and retirement plans. The lack of these essential safeguards can leave gig workers vulnerable, particularly in times of economic downturn or personal crises.

The challenge for governments is to create a regulatory framework that acknowledges the unique nature of gig work while providing a safety net for these workers. Some countries and regions are beginning to address this, with policies aimed at extending certain benefits to gig workers. However, progress is uneven and often caught in legal and bureaucratic complexities. The debate frequently centers around the balance between maintaining flexibility, which is a hallmark of gig work, and ensuring fair labor standards and protections.

The traditional tax structure is often ill-suited to the irregular income patterns of gig workers, leading to tax collection and compliance challenges. Moreover, as more people shift to gig work, contributions to social security systems may decrease, potentially impacting the sustainability of these programs.

While the gig and freelance economy offer numerous opportunities for workers and businesses alike, the lag in governmental regulation and benefits provision is a growing concern. There is a pressing need for updated laws and policies that reflect the changing nature of work. This modernization would protect the rights and well-being of gig workers and ensure the continued growth and sustainability of this vital sector of the economy. Governments must act swiftly and thoughtfully to bridge this regulatory gap, ensuring that the evolution of work is supported by an equally evolved legal and social framework.

When contemplating the impact of remote work and freelancing, a crucial aspect that both corporations and governments must consider is its potential effect on the global carbon footprint. These employment models, predominantly reliant on remote operations, offer a unique opportunity to contribute significantly to environmental sustainability. This consideration is particularly vital in the context of escalating concerns about climate change and the pressing need for effective measures to reduce carbon emissions worldwide. The evolving landscape of remote work, significantly influenced by the global pandemic, has ignited a conversation about its potential impact on sustainability and reducing carbon footprints. This discussion becomes even more interesting when we see companies aiming for big goals like zero carbon emissions, but at the same time, they are slow to fully adopt remote work. The contradiction lies in the overlooked potential of remote work as a powerful tool in the sustainability arsenal.

A key aspect of remote work's environmental impact is its ability to diminish the necessity for daily commutes. According to the Global Work-from-Home Experience Survey[11], conducted in 2020, the shift to remote work during the pandemic led to a 14% reduction in global commuting. The U.S. Environmental Protection Agency estimates that transportation contributes about 29% of total greenhouse gas emissions[12], making it the largest contributor in the country. The reduction in commuting not only lessens traffic congestion but also significantly curtails carbon emissions and air pollution. Complementing this, a study by Cornell and Microsoft[13] found that remote workers could have a 54% lower carbon footprint compared to onsite workers. It was also noted that hybrid workers, who work from home two to four days per week, could reduce their carbon footprint by 11% to 29%. This is significant, considering the U.S. Environmental Protection Agency's statistic that transportation accounts for about 29% of total U.S. greenhouse gas emissions, making it the largest contributor in the country. Reducing commuting through remote work directly impacts this statistic, offering a clear pathway toward sustainability goals. Governments have a pivotal role in fostering this transition. Policies encouraging remote work can be instrumental in achieving broader sustainability goals. For instance, the European Union's Green Deal aims to make Europe the first climate-neutral continent by 2050, and remote work can be a vital component of this vision. Providing incentives for companies to adopt remote work arrangements and investing in digital infrastructure to support telecommuting are ways governments can promote this cause. Companies, for their part, must recognize the close relationship between remote work and sustainability. By reducing the need for large office spaces and the associated energy consumption, companies not only lower their carbon footprint but also align with evolving workforce preferences for flexibility and work-life balance.

The promotion of remote work by companies and governments aligns with the urgent need to address environmental concerns and the evolving expectations of the modern workforce. The reduction in commuting alone offers a substantial opportunity to decrease carbon emissions, making remote work an underutilized yet potent tool in the fight against climate change. This alignment of environmental goals with the preferences of a modern, connected workforce can foster a more sustainable and productive future.

In the following chapters, we will explore the concept of navigating the unknown from various angles, providing the reader with the necessary context, methodologies, and insights they seek.

The book commences by examining how the COVID-19 pandemic has reshaped leadership dynamics, distinguishing between genuine leaders, future-of-work leaders, and pretenders. This leads to an exploration of the evolving role of leadership in remote work and gig-freelancer environments. Next, the book reveals **care** as the most crucial element for modern work setups. This is followed by a deep dive into the significant impact of the COVID-19 pandemic on global professional landscapes, focusing on the shift towards remote work and the vital role of leadership skills in adapting to these changes. I then present examples of how a change in leadership can alter the direction of an entire organization, for better or worse. This segues into a discussion on the differences between management and leadership in local and remote team setups. The book then showcases a variety of proven practices that modern leadership can leverage to generate extraordinary outcomes for organizations and gig-freelancer and remote workers. This is followed by the provision of tactics for leaders of modern work setups to effectively lead multi-generational organizations. The book concludes by emphasizing the importance of new leaders staying abreast of technological advances to excel in the new world of leadership. This structure provides a comprehensive exploration of modern leadership in the context of changing work environments, offering valuable insights and practical strategies for those aspiring to lead in this new era.

"You don't lead by hitting people over the head – that is assault, not leadership."
Dwight D. Eisenhower

Pandemic Pressure: Distinguishing True Leaders from Pretenders

The COVID-19 pandemic served as a multifaceted learning experience, influencing areas ranging from remote work practices to a deeper appreciation of life and freedom. It also catalyzed new business opportunities and sparked innovation. In this chapter, we will explore a particularly intriguing aspect of the pandemic: its role as a revelatory force in leadership and management.

During the transition to remote work, the pandemic inadvertently became a benchmark test for authentic leadership. This shift illuminated the strengths and weaknesses of those in managerial roles. Previously, traditional office environments may have allowed some individuals to project an image of effective leadership, supported, in part, by conventional management literature and practices. However, with its unique challenges, the remote work environment required a more genuine embodiment of leadership qualities.

The pandemic environment revealed that true leadership extends beyond mere appearances or textbook strategies. It underscored the significance of adaptability, empathy, and genuine engagement with team members, particularly in times of uncertainty. In essence, the pandemic stripped away the veneer of performative management, highlighting the importance of sincere, caring leadership. This transformation in the workplace is critical, reflecting on how it reshaped our understanding of what it truly means to lead and manage effectively.

In the heart of Bilbao, Spain, where I found myself confined unexpectedly during the pandemic; it felt like living in a bubble, cut off from the world and everyone in it, week after seemingly unending week. My wife was 600 kilometers (about 372 miles) away in Valencia, working remotely, and our children were suddenly studying remotely. It was not just us; this thing hit everyone, everywhere, with the rules and restrictions changing depending on where you were.

I observed numerous managers, who perhaps lacked certain leadership qualities, facing difficulties adjusting to the new reality of remote work. This struggle to adapt was not just a personal challenge for them, but it also had a palpable impact on their teams and the wider organization. As the work environment transitioned to remote settings, the differences between mere management and true leadership became more apparent. These managers, who might have been effective in traditional office settings, found it challenging to maintain the same level of effectiveness in a remote context. Their teams, and consequently the organizations, experienced the effects of this transition, highlighting the need for adaptable and empathetic leadership skills in the evolving workplace landscape.

Observations from a neutral perspective during the pandemic revealed significant insights about leadership. The crisis illuminated the actions of prominent figures, often referred to as leaders, and the results were not always commendable. It is relatively easy to make grand statements, but true leadership is tested when faced with adversity. Unfortunately, many did not meet the expectations associated with their roles. This situation underscores the importance of effective leadership in times of crisis.

The pandemic presented unique challenges and opportunities, and it was in navigating these that the defining qualities of genuine leadership versus basic management came to the forefront. My focused observations during this time have shed light on these key differences, helping to understand what separates effective, inspiring leaders from those who simply manage tasks and operations.

Let us now delve into the distinguishing factors that, in my view and based on my observations, set true leaders apart from mere managers during the pandemic. These elements, which became particularly evident during this period, offer insights into the contrasting approaches and capabilities of individuals in leadership roles.

Adaptability, as a cornerstone of leadership, especially during the COVID-19 pandemic, took on an unprecedented level of importance. This period was marked by rapid, often unpredictable changes, requiring leaders to evolve almost in real time. The pandemic did not offer the luxury of static decision-making or rigid adherence to pre-existing strategies; instead, it demanded a fluid, dynamic approach to leadership.

The pandemic illuminated the need for leaders to possess a keen awareness of their environment. This awareness was not just about keeping abreast of the latest developments in the pandemic's progression; it extended into a deeper understanding of how these changes were affecting the people they led, the overall industry landscape, and the broader societal context.

What set truly adaptable leaders apart was their ability to react to change and anticipate and prepare for it. This proactive adaptation was not about predicting the future with precision but about creating systems and cultures that could pivot quickly and effectively. It involved a mindset that embraced change as an integral part of the leadership journey rather than a disruptive force to be resisted.

Another critical aspect of adaptability highlighted by the pandemic was emotional flexibility. Leaders had to manage not only their own stress and uncertainty but also that of their team members during the pandemic. They had to balance maintaining a vision for the future by addressing the very real and immediate concerns of their people. This required a blend of emotional intelligence and resilience, enabling leaders to remain grounded and composed, offering stability and reassurance to their teams.

Moreover, adaptable leaders during the pandemic demonstrated an exceptional ability to learn and unlearn. They recognized that strategies and skills that worked in a pre-pandemic world might not be as effective in the new reality. This learning agility, being open to new ideas, willing to let go of outdated practices, and being able to rapidly acquire new skills, was a vital component of successful leadership during this period.

Adaptability in leadership during the COVID-19 pandemic was about more than just tactical shifts or strategic pivots. It was about embodying a mindset of flexibility, emotional resilience, anticipatory thinking, and continuous learning. It was about seeing change not as a barrier but as a pathway to innovation and growth, both for leaders themselves and the people they guide. This perspective on leadership, shaped by the trials of the pandemic, has laid the foundation for a new paradigm in how we approach change and uncertainty in the ever-evolving landscape of the modern world.

Empathetic communication, particularly highlighted during the COVID-19 pandemic, became a fundamental aspect of effective leadership. This period was not just a health crisis; it was a complex mosaic of personal, professional, and societal challenges that deeply affected individuals and communities.

Empathy in leadership during this time transcended the conventional understanding of the term. It was not merely about understanding or sharing the feelings of others; it was about deeply integrating this understanding into every communication made and decision taken. The pandemic era placed leaders in a position where they had to connect with their teams as professionals and as human beings facing a collective adversity.

This form of communication involved active listening, a skill that became indispensable, a skill that many managers lack. Leaders had to listen not just to respond or instruct, but to genuinely understand their team members' fears, challenges, and uncertainties their team members were experiencing. This listening extended beyond work-related issues to encompass the broader emotional and psychological well-being of their teams.

But empathetic communication was more than just listening; it was also about responding in a way that validated these experiences. Leaders had to find ways to acknowledge the struggles, provide support, and adapt workplace expectations in light of the unprecedented circumstances. This required a delicate balance, maintaining productivity and focus while being flexible and understanding of the varied personal situations team members were dealing with.

Moreover, empathetic communication during the pandemic also meant being transparent and authentic. Leaders had to communicate not just the what and the how but also the why behind decisions and changes. This transparency helped in building trust and understanding, even when the news was difficult or the decisions were tough.

In the span of my career, which includes roles in both local and remote teams, small enterprises, and larger corporations, I have rarely encountered leaders or managers who truly exemplify authenticity and transparency. It has always intrigued me why some Human Resources training prioritizes the concept of being "diplomatically appropriate" over encouraging managers to remain genuine, of course, within the parameters of respect and professionalism. This realization has prompted me to reflect on the nuances of workplace communication and the equilibrium between authenticity and maintaining professional norms in diverse organizational cultures.

Perhaps one of the most significant aspects of empathetic communication during this time was its role in fostering a sense of community and belonging. With teams dispersed and working remotely, creating a sense of connection and togetherness was more challenging yet more crucial than ever. Empathetic leaders were those who could bridge the physical gap with emotional and communicative closeness, making each team member feel seen, heard, and valued.

Empathetic communication in the context of the pandemic was an amalgamation of active listening, responsive and supportive dialogue, transparency, authenticity, and a profound commitment to fostering community. It was about leaders stepping into the shoes of their team members, not just to walk a mile in them, which frequently happens with managers rather than leaders, but also to pave a path forward together in those trying times. This approach to leadership communication has not only been essential for navigating the pandemic but has also set a new standard for how leaders engage with their teams in any challenging situation.

Resilience, as it emerged in the context of leadership during the COVID-19 pandemic, took on a profound and multifaceted significance. This period, characterized by relentless uncertainty and frequent setbacks, demanded from leaders a form of resilience that was both deeply personal and expansively influential.

During the pandemic, resilience was not merely about bouncing back; it was about growing through challenges and adversity. Leaders faced the task of steering their organizations through turbulent economic and operational waters and being a beacon of stability and hope for their teams.

This brand of resilience was deeply rooted in a mindset that embraced change and uncertainty not as insurmountable obstacles but as a catalyst for growth and innovation. It involved maintaining a long-term vision even when short-term challenges seemed overwhelming. Leaders had to project a sense of calm and assurance, instilling confidence in their teams even when they themselves were navigating uncharted waters.

But resilience during the pandemic was also about showing vulnerability, which a classical manager would mostly avoid. Leaders who authentically shared their own challenges and uncertainties were able to forge deeper connections with their team members, creating a shared sense of journey and struggle. This vulnerability was not a sign of weakness but a powerful tool for building trust and solidarity.

Furthermore, resilience in this context was closely linked to adaptability. Leaders had to constantly reassess and adjust their strategies to the rapidly evolving landscape. This adaptability was not just a tactical necessity but a core component of resilience, the ability to stay agile and responsive in the face of change.

Leaders also played a crucial role in fostering resilience within their teams. They had to empower their team members, encouraging them to develop their own resilience. This involved creating an environment where taking calculated risks, learning from failures, and supporting each other was the norm.

Resilience during the COVID-19 pandemic was about leaders embodying a blend of steadfastness and flexibility, vision and vulnerability, strength and empathy. It was about leading not just with a strategic mind but with a human heart, recognizing that true resilience in leadership is as much about uplifting others as it is about standing strong. This understanding of resilience has reshaped the expectations and ideals of leadership in times of crisis and beyond.

Digital proficiency, a crucial leadership attribute that gained unprecedented importance during the COVID-19 pandemic, represented far more than just a technical skill set. This period of extensive remote work and digital reliance demanded from leaders not only an understanding of technological tools but also a deeper comprehension of how to lead effectively in a virtual environment.

In this context, the essence of digital proficiency went beyond mere familiarity with video conferencing software or project management tools. It was about leveraging technology to maintain and even enhance the connectivity and productivity of teams dispersed by the pandemic. Leaders had to know how to choose the right tools to facilitate communication, collaboration, and workflow management in a landscape where the traditional office structure had been upended.

However, the core of digital proficiency during the pandemic lay in the human aspect of technology usage. Leaders were called upon to navigate the subtleties of remote team dynamics: fostering engagement, ensuring inclusivity, and maintaining team morale in a digital space. This required a nuanced understanding of how technology could bridge physical distance, creating a virtual environment that was as conducive to collaboration and team spirit as a physical office.

Moreover, digital proficiency meant being able to lead by example in the virtual domain. Leaders had to be visibly present in digital channels, demonstrating their commitment to this new mode of work. This visibility helped in establishing a sense of normalcy and continuity in a time fraught with disruptions and uncertainties.

Digital proficiency for leaders during the pandemic also entailed an element of digital empathy. Understanding that team members might have varied levels of comfort and expertise with digital tools, leaders needed to be patient and supportive, providing resources and training to ease the transition to remote work.

Leaders with high digital proficiency also recognized the importance of digital well-being. They were mindful of the potential for digital fatigue among their teams and sought to establish healthy boundaries and practices to prevent burnout in a world where work and home spaces had merged.

Digital proficiency during the COVID-19 pandemic was a composite of technical skill, adaptability, and a deep understanding of the human experience in a digital world. It was about using technology not just as a means to an end but as a vital enabler of effective, empathetic, and inclusive leadership. This refined understanding of digital proficiency has indelibly marked the future of leadership in an increasingly digitalized world.

One leader I admire told me, "We need to be even more human in this digital world, and especially during the pandemic."

Transparency and honesty in leadership, particularly highlighted during the COVID-19 pandemic, assumed a critical role in navigating the crisis. This period, fraught with uncertainty and rapid changes, placed an extraordinary emphasis on the need for leaders to cultivate trust and credibility through open and honest communication. How could we create and foster trust within a community that consisted of hundreds of gig workers, freelancers, and remote workers? A tricky thing to achieve but not impossible.

During the pandemic, transparency was not just about conveying information; it was about sharing knowledge and insights in a way that was both accessible and meaningful to diverse audiences. Leaders faced the complex task of communicating about evolving challenges, often with incomplete information, while ensuring that their messages fostered clarity rather than confusion. This required a careful balance, offering honesty about the difficulties faced without inducing undue alarm.

In a global environment, the success of communication does not just rely on the leader who initiated it but also on the remote individuals who come from various cultures and ideologies. This complexity has made transparency and trust more challenging to achieve.

Honesty, in this context, extended beyond the factual accuracy of information. It encompassed a genuineness in acknowledging the limitations of what was known, the challenges ahead, and the potential impact on the organization and its people. This kind of honesty was instrumental in building trust, a commodity of immense value in times of crisis.

Transparency and honesty were not just crisis management tools; they were essential in maintaining morale and engagement. By openly addressing the realities of the situation, leaders could align their teams around shared challenges and objectives, fostering a sense of unity and purpose. This open communication helped demystify the crisis, making it more manageable and less intimidating for everyone involved.

However, effective transparency and honesty required more than just open communication; it required empathy and sensitivity. Leaders had to be mindful of how information was delivered, ensuring that it was done with consideration for the diverse emotional and psychological states of their audience. This empathetic approach helped mitigate anxiety and provided a sense of security and support.

In addition, transparent and honest leaders during the pandemic were those who encouraged dialogue and feedback. They understood that communication was a two-way street, and by fostering an environment where questions, concerns, and ideas could be openly shared, they strengthened their teams' collective resilience and adaptability.

Transparency and honesty during the COVID-19 pandemic were about much more than just the dissemination of information. They were about building a foundation of trust, credibility, and collective strength, grounded in an authentic, empathetic, and inclusive approach to leadership communication. This open and honest leadership paradigm has set a precedent that will likely influence organizational cultures far beyond the pandemic.

Innovative problem-solving, as a leadership attribute, was dramatically magnified in importance during the COVID-19 pandemic. This era, marked by unprecedented challenges and a rapidly evolving landscape, required leaders to embrace innovation not as a mere buzzword but as a fundamental approach to overcoming obstacles and seizing opportunities.

The pandemic's unique problems required creativity and out-of-the-box thinking that went beyond conventional strategies. Leaders were confronted with situations that had no playbook or historical precedent. This demanded not only the capacity to think creatively but also the courage to venture into untested waters, making decisions that could chart new courses for their organizations.

Innovative problem-solving in this context was characterized by a willingness to experiment and learn. Leaders had to foster environments where trial and error were part of the journey, where risks were taken, and where failures were seen as stepping stones to success. This approach required cultivating a culture of curiosity and openness, where team members felt empowered to bring forward new ideas and explore alternative solutions.

Moreover, innovative leadership during the pandemic meant breaking down traditional silos and encouraging cross-functional collaboration. The complexity and multi-dimensional nature of the challenges required a diverse range of perspectives and expertise. Leaders who facilitated this collaborative innovation saw more robust and holistic solutions emerge.

Importantly, innovative problem-solving during this time also involved leveraging technology and digital tools in novel ways. The sudden shift to remote work and the need for social distancing accelerated digital transformation in many organizations. Leaders had to quickly adapt to these technologies, not just for operational continuity but as platforms for innovative ways of working, communicating, and delivering value.

Additionally, this period highlighted the need for leaders to have a keen sense of situational awareness to understand the broader context in which they were operating. Innovative solutions were not developed in a vacuum but were responsive to the changing needs of customers, employees, and the broader community.

Innovative problem-solving during the COVID-19 pandemic was about much more than coming up with new ideas; it was about creating a culture where innovation thrived, risks were managed intelligently, and creativity was harnessed to navigate through a landscape of uncertainty. This approach to leadership was not only instrumental in dealing with the immediate crisis but has also paved the way for more agile, resilient, and forward-thinking organizations in the future.

Emotional intelligence, as a leadership quality, gained an extraordinary level of significance during the COVID-19 pandemic. This era, fraught with global upheaval, personal and professional challenges, and a pervasive sense of uncertainty, called for leaders who could navigate not just the logistical aspects of this crisis but its emotional landscape as well.

In this context, emotional intelligence was about much more than the ability to understand and manage one's own emotions. It extended to a profound understanding of and empathy for the emotions of others. Leaders faced the complex task of steering their teams through not just a business or economic crisis but an emotional and psychological one. This demanded a deepened sensitivity to the varied emotional responses of their team members and a commitment to supporting them through these challenges.

I've observed numerous managers who regrettably possess minimal emotional intelligence overseeing local teams. This is a stark contrast to their proficiency in technical skills such as Excel and PowerPoint, which are especially prevalent in large and multinational organizations. In my professional opinion, the ability to effectively manage both local and remote teams with a strong sense of emotional intelligence is a cornerstone of authentic leadership. This skill set should be a priority in our assessment criteria, ensuring that we are not just appointing managers but true leaders who can inspire and lead teams, regardless of their physical location.

The pandemic highlighted leaders' need to demonstrate empathy, patience, and compassion. These qualities were essential in creating a supportive and understanding work environment where team members felt valued and cared for, not just as employees but as human beings dealing with a shared global crisis.

Besides, emotional intelligence during this period involved a heightened level of self-awareness. Leaders had to be aware of their emotional states and how these could impact their decision-making, communication, and team interactions. The ability to remain composed, think clearly, and exhibit calmness in the face of adversity was crucial. This composure provided a sense of stability and reassurance to teams navigating through uncertainty.

Leaders with high emotional intelligence were also adept at managing stress and preventing burnout, both for themselves and their teams. They recognized the signs of emotional fatigue and took proactive steps to address them, such as encouraging breaks, promoting work-life balance, and providing resources for mental and emotional well-being.

Furthermore, emotional intelligence in leadership during the pandemic meant being able to foster an environment of psychological safety. This involved creating a space where team members felt comfortable sharing their concerns, challenges, and ideas without fear of judgment or retribution. Such an environment encouraged openness, bolstered team cohesion, and facilitated more effective problem-solving and innovation.

Emotional intelligence in the era of COVID-19 was a blend of empathy, self-awareness, and mindful leadership. It was about leading with the heart as well as the mind, recognizing the human element in every aspect of the crisis. This approach not only helped organizations navigate through the pandemic but also set a new benchmark for empathetic and emotionally intelligent leadership in the face of any challenge.

My understanding of emotional intelligence is deeply informed by extensive research and observation. The notion that emotional intelligence is an inherent trait rather than solely a learned skill emerges from several key observations.

Firstly, the roots of emotional intelligence often appear in early childhood. Long before formal education shapes a child's abilities, certain children exhibit natural tendencies towards empathy, self-awareness, and managing emotions. This early display suggests an innate component to emotional intelligence, independent of external teaching or experience.

Furthermore, emotional intelligence is intricately tied to an individual's temperament and personality, factors largely considered to be innate. Certain personalities are predisposed to higher levels of empathy or emotional regulation. This intrinsic link implies that while emotional intelligence can be nurtured and developed, its foundational elements are often present from birth.

Genetic studies bolster this view. Research, particularly involving twins, indicates a genetic basis for aspects of emotional intelligence. Identical twins often show more closely aligned levels of emotional intelligence compared to fraternal twins, suggesting that genetics play a significant role in determining one's emotional capabilities.

Additionally, the natural emotional responses exhibited by individuals, including the intuitive understanding of and reaction to others' emotions, further point towards an inherent aspect of emotional intelligence. These responses are often untaught and spontaneous, indicating an innate ability rather than a solely acquired skill.

Lastly, the universality of certain emotional responses across cultures also suggests an innate basis. While cultural factors undeniably shape emotional expression and understanding, the core ability to recognize and empathize with emotions is a universal human trait, hinting at a biological and inherent foundation.

While learning and experience can undoubtedly enhance emotional intelligence, its roots appear to be significantly influenced by innate factors, including genetics, personality, and early childhood development. Hence the importance of selecting the right people to lead, especially in organizations that now or soon will become remote organizations encompassing gig and freelance workers.

Decisive action, as a leadership quality, was immensely magnified in its importance during the COVID-19 pandemic. In a landscape dominated by uncertainty and rapid change, the ability of leaders to make informed, timely decisions became a crucial determinant of an organization's ability to navigate the crisis effectively. Nowadays, we clearly see that uncertainty is not something proper to a pandemic anymore.

During the pandemic, decisiveness in leadership took on a nuanced character. It was not simply about making quick decisions; it was about making the right decisions quickly. Leaders were required to process a constant influx of information, some conflicting or evolving, and express this into clear, actionable strategies. This required a balance of pace and thoughtfulness, ensuring that decisions were both prompt and well considered.

The pandemic also highlighted the importance of decisiveness in crisis management. In situations where delays could have significant consequences, the ability to act swiftly and confidently was paramount. However, this decisiveness was not about being inflexible; effective leaders were also open to adjusting their decisions as new information and feedback became available. This adaptability was a key part of being decisive in an environment where the only constant was change.

Moreover, decisive action during this time was closely linked to clarity of communication. Leaders needed to articulate their decisions and the rationale behind them clearly and effectively, ensuring that their teams understood the direction and the reasons for it. This clarity helped in rallying teams around a common purpose, even amidst the turbulence of the pandemic.

Decisive leaders also demonstrated a deep understanding of their organization's values and priorities, which guided their decision-making. In a time when difficult choices had to be made, such as budget cuts or shifts in operations, having a solid grasp of what was fundamentally important to the organization helped in making decisions that were aligned with its long-term vision and integrity.

Furthermore, decisive leadership in the context of the pandemic involved a level of courage. Leaders had to make tough calls, sometimes with limited data and often with significant implications. The willingness to take responsibility for these decisions, to stand by them, and to navigate their consequences was proof of the strength and conviction of effective leaders.

Decisive action during the COVID-19 pandemic was a complex interplay of rapid decision-making, adaptability, clear communication, value-driven judgment, and courage. This approach to leadership was not just about guiding organizations through a crisis but also about setting a precedent for how to lead with decisiveness in any uncertain and fast-changing environment.

Inclusive leadership, as a critical attribute, gained profound significance during the COVID-19 pandemic. This period, marked by global disruption and uncertainty, cast a spotlight on the need for leaders to embrace and champion diversity and inclusiveness in their approach to navigating the crisis.

Inclusive leadership in the context of the pandemic was about much more than acknowledging diversity within teams. It was about actively seeking out, valuing, and leveraging the different perspectives, experiences, and skills that each team member brought to the table. The varied challenges posed by the pandemic, from remote work setups to personal hardships, affected individuals in different ways, highlighting the importance of understanding and addressing these diverse experiences.

Leaders who excelled in inclusivity during this time demonstrated a keen awareness of the unique needs and circumstances of their team members. They understood that policies and decisions could not be one-size-fits-all but needed to consider the varying impacts on different groups. This sensitivity was crucial in ensuring that all team members felt supported and valued, irrespective of their personal situations.

Inclusive leaders were also proactive in creating environments where all voices were heard and respected. They recognized that the best solutions often come from a multitude of perspectives, and they actively encouraged participation and dialogue from all members of their teams. This approach not only fostered a more creative and collaborative problem-solving environment but also built a stronger sense of belonging and community among team members.

Moreover, inclusive leadership during the pandemic meant being attuned to potential biases and barriers that could hinder inclusivity. Leaders had to be vigilant against unconscious biases in decision-making, communication, and the allocation of opportunities and resources. They also needed to be aware of and address any systemic issues within their organizations that could perpetuate inequality.

Another important aspect of inclusive leadership in this context was empathy. Leaders had to not only understand the diverse experiences of their team members but also empathize with them. This empathy was vital in building trust and ensuring that every team member felt valued and understood, which in turn enhanced engagement and productivity.

Inclusive leadership during the COVID-19 pandemic was about recognizing the strength that lies in diversity and actively cultivating an environment where this diversity could thrive. It was about leading with a deep respect for the individuality of each team member and a commitment to ensuring that everyone had the opportunity to contribute and succeed. This approach to leadership not only helped organizations navigate the pandemic more effectively but also set a new standard for how inclusivity is integral to effective leadership in any context.

Vision and purpose in leadership, particularly accentuated during the COVID-19 pandemic, emerged as critical elements for guiding organizations through an era of unprecedented challenges. The pandemic, bringing with it a landscape of uncertainty and rapid change, underscored the need for leaders to provide a clear and compelling direction that could anchor and motivate their teams.

In this context, having a vision was about more than setting long-term goals; it was about articulating a meaningful path forward during confusion and upheaval. Leaders with a strong vision were those who could look beyond the immediate crisis and envisage a future that inspired hope and resilience. They were able to paint a picture of what lay beyond the pandemic, offering a sense of optimism and possibility even in dark times.

But vision during the pandemic was not just about looking ahead. It was also about ensuring that this vision was deeply connected to a sense of purpose. Leaders were called upon to reinforce the why behind what their organizations did, connecting day-to-day activities to a larger mission. This connection to a greater purpose was crucial in maintaining engagement and motivation when external motivators, like office environments or traditional work routines, were disrupted.

Moreover, compelling vision and purpose in leadership during this time involved aligning these ideals with the evolving realities and needs of both the organization and its stakeholders. Leaders had to be attuned to how the pandemic was changing the world and adapt their vision accordingly. This adaptability ensured that their vision remained relevant and resonant, even as circumstances evolved.

Effective leaders also communicated their vision and purpose with clarity and consistency. In a time when confusion was rampant, clear communication about the direction and the reasons behind it helped in creating a sense of stability and confidence. Leaders who could effectively articulate their vision fostered a shared understanding and commitment among their teams, aligning efforts towards common goals.

Furthermore, leaders with a strong vision and sense of purpose demonstrated an ability to engage and mobilize their teams around these ideals. They inspired action not just through directives but through the power of a shared vision, creating a collaborative environment where every team member felt they were contributing to something meaningful.

Vision and purpose during the COVID-19 pandemic were about providing a beacon of direction in a storm of uncertainty. They were about leading with one eye on the horizon and one hand on the heart, guiding organizations not just through survival but toward a future imbued with hope, meaning, and resilience. This approach to leadership not only proved essential during the pandemic but also set a precedent for how vision and purpose can serve as foundational pillars in navigating any complex and uncertain environment.

During my tenure leading my organizations, our guiding vision was always centered around collaborative efforts to achieve exceptional business results. This focus aimed at expanding our reach and delivery capabilities, thereby reaching a wider audience. The ripple effect of this expansion was the creation of more job opportunities globally, with a specific emphasis on remote geographies and communities that are often underrepresented.

There were moments when I was a silent observer in team meetings, and I would hear our team members speak about this vision. Hearing them articulate the goals and ideals that we held so dear always filled me with immense pride. At times, it was so moving that it brought tears to my eyes, a testament to the emotional connection I felt to our vision and the people working tirelessly to bring it to fruition.

For me, as a person, purpose is everything. Living your purpose, explaining it transparently, and bringing people who believe in the same purpose together has been vital in my more than 35 years of career and remote team leadership.

"In the realm of ideas, everything depends on enthusiasm; in the real world, all rests on perseverance."
Johann Wolfgang von Goethe

The Art of Leading a Global, Remote, Gig-Freelancer Driven Workforce

In today's rapidly evolving professional landscape, the significance of leadership skills has never been more pronounced. As we witness a significant shift towards gig-based, freelance, and remote work environments, the necessity for adept leadership becomes increasingly crucial. This transformation underscores the importance of being able to navigate the unique challenges and opportunities presented by these modern work setups. Effective leadership in this context is not just an asset but a vital component in ensuring success and adaptability in a world where traditional work structures are being redefined and decentralized.

While it is entirely feasible to structure work using Artificial Intelligence (AI) and streamline operations with sophisticated apps, this approach only scratches the surface. It essentially boils down to organizing tasks and expecting humans to function like automatons, focused solely on hitting targets. This method lacks the essence of leadership, the sense of community, shared objectives, and a unifying purpose beyond mere financial gain.

Imagine leadership as a journey with different routes. In the context of nations and armies, think of a leader who speaks to people with shared historical experiences. This leader guides by culture and tradition. The team is disciplined, the structure is clear, and life follows a routine of rituals and ceremonies. Here, care is shown by protecting the legacy and promising a shared future. This leader, like a guide, creates a supportive environment for its people. They invest in preservation and mentorship, viewing every member as a long-term partner in a shared venture. Care here involves feedback sessions, team-building retreats, and recognition of milestones.

Now, imagine a busy corporation where activity is constant. Here, the leader is both a coach and a manager, coordinating a diverse set of skills and personalities. This leader creates a supportive company culture for its people. They focus on growth and mentorship and view every employee as a long-term collaborator in a shared project. Care here involves feedback sessions, team-building activities, and acknowledging both personal and professional achievements.

Finally, let's look at the dynamic world of gig workers in a remote work system, a mix of independent individuals, each with their own rhythm. Leadership here is like guiding ships at night. The temporary nature of gig work means the leader must work harder to guide, building connections among changing faces. Care is more about making each interaction meaningful, acknowledging each person's individuality. It is about creating short but real moments of connection, ensuring that everyone feels acknowledged and valued. In this context, the essence of leadership changes with the environment. For the leader, it is about respecting and nurturing a shared identity; for corporate executives, it is about developing a culture and deep roots; and for the leader of freelancers, it is about mastering the art of brief but impactful encounters. Each leader must understand their domain and choose the methods and tone that best resonate with their unique group of individuals.

Leading gig workers or freelancers is like being the caretaker of a large and diverse garden, where each plant is a unique individual, flourishing in its own specific environment. The freelancer leader's task is not to create uniformity but to nurture diversity, ensuring that everyone can thrive in their own way. They must become adept at the art of remote conversations that cross time zones, languages, and cultural nuances, often relying on the written word where much can be lost in translation. This leader's compass must be finely tuned to navigate the complexities of schedules that never quite align and the motivations that are as varied as the stars. They must become fluent in the language of flexibility, translating organizational goals into personal ones that resonate with a freelancer's own ambitions and lifestyle. It is a dance of diplomacy and strategy, where each step is carefully chosen to respect autonomy while gently guiding towards a shared outcome.

Contrast this with the leader of an army or a nation, whose followers often share a common rhythm, the march of boots on the ground, the anthem that unites, and the flag that flies for all. These leaders can draw on collective memories and a sense of duty that has been instilled over lifetimes. Their words can stir a collective heart, and their vision can become a shared horizon towards which an entire population moves. The leader of a remote team or gig team, however, must learn to touch the heart of a mosaic, each piece with its own pulse. Their vision must be multifaceted, a prism that can refract a single goal into a spectrum of individual aspirations. It is a delicate balance to strike, requiring a depth of empathy and an unwavering commitment to inclusiveness. The main difference lies in the continuity of engagement and the basis of the relationship. In an army or nation, the leader and the follower are bound by a continuity of service and the permanence of their roles. They are part of an ongoing narrative.

For the freelancer, each project could be seen as a full story, with a start and a finish. The individual leading a freelance organization doesn't rely on a shared history but must be constructed and reconstructed with every new task and every new team member. In this constantly changing environment, the leader's role is not so much about giving orders but more about making things easier, not so much about controlling but more about bringing together. It is about creating consistency in a situation that is naturally marked by change. The challenge is not just in the leadership itself but in the continuous adjustment needed to meet each freelancer where they are, transforming a group of individual performers into a harmonious ensemble without lessening the beauty of each individual contribution.

In a world increasingly defined by polarization, the task of leading, truly leading, not just managing, a diverse group of freelancers toward a common corporate goal becomes a study of balance and sensitivity. This leader must be a cartographer of human landscapes, understanding the divides and crafting bridges with careful, deliberate steps. First and foremost, this leader practices the art of active listening, not just hearing but truly understanding the unique perspectives each freelancer brings to the table. In a polarized environment, every voice holds a piece of the puzzle, and every perspective can shed light on a facet of the truth. They know that care is not a one-size-fits-all solution; it must be tailored to resonate with the individual's values, aspirations, and cultural background. This leader must be a visionary, painting a picture of a common goal that is not just a corporate milestone but a beacon that aligns with the freelancers' personal ambitions. They must articulate this shared objective in a way that transcends geographical, political, and ideological divides, finding common ground that respects and values the differences each freelancer brings. In practical terms, leading in a polarized world means embracing diversity as a strength rather than a hurdle. It means nurturing an environment where debates are encouraged but anchored in mutual respect and a shared commitment to the organization's success. It calls for transparency and consistency in communication, ensuring that no matter where a freelancer is in the world, they feel connected to the core of the organization.

This style of leadership also demands an unparalleled level of emotional intelligence. The leader must be adept at recognizing and navigating the emotional undercurrents that polarization can bring to the surface. They must act as a mediator, a negotiator, and, at times, a peacekeeper, always striving to align individual passions with the collective mission. To lead gig-freelancers spread across the planet, this leader must also be a champion of inclusion, ensuring that each member of the team, regardless of their location or viewpoint, has equal access to opportunities and a voice in decisions that affect their work. They must be flag-bearers for the culture of care, demonstrating through actions that they value each freelancer not just as a contributor to the corporate engine but as a human being with goals and dreams of their own.

Ultimately, the challenge lies in crafting a shared narrative, one that weaves through the tapestry of polarization and creates a story where each freelancer can find their chapter. This narrative acknowledges and respects individual goals while elevating the collective aim as a worthy, unifying quest, a quest that promises not just corporate success but personal fulfillment and growth.

In this global dance, the leader is both conductor and audience, aware that the music is a blend of different notes and rhythms, each essential, each cherished. It is a leadership style that celebrates diversity, champions empathy and recognizes that in the heart of polarization lies the potential for a richer, more nuanced harmony. In a world where division and disagreement are growing, and where prejudice, rejection, and sadly, even hatred, are making it harder for us to stay connected, there is a big question: How does one navigate the helm of leadership when the crew is scattered across the globe? How does one unify a multitude, diverse in culture, faith, sexuality, and ideology, into not just a team but a community that doesn't just operate but thrives, setting sail toward extraordinary business horizons?

"I have learned that people will forget what you said, people will forget what you did, but people will never forget how you made them feel."
Maya Angelou

Beyond Command and Control: Embracing Caring as the Keystone of Leadership

Throughout my career, I have had the unique opportunity to immerse myself in a multitude of companies, each characterized by their distinct style of leadership. This journey has been nothing short of enlightening, leading me to an intriguing realization. Despite my consistent personality, these varied leadership approaches have consistently managed to extract the best out of me. This could very well be attributed to my own adaptability; I might possess a higher-than-average ability to adjust and thrive under different leadership styles. Or it is a trait innate to my character, allowing me to seamlessly blend into varying leadership environments. Despite the variety of experiences, a clear common feature among exceptional groups and organizations is their focus on caring. Caring leadership stands out as a critical quality in the best teams and organizations I have seen. I fervently believe that many of you may perceive caring as simply nurturing a community, organization, or group. Yet, my perspective on this is profoundly different and deeply passionate. To me, caring transcends the utmost pinnacle of human quality. It eclipses love, overshadows passion, surpasses knowledge, and even outstrips academic achievements. I cannot stress enough that the highest epitome of human quality is, unequivocally, caring.

But let us delve deeper. Caring is not confined to just the individuals who work for you or with you in an organization or community. Its scope is vastly more expansive. It encompasses caring for customers, your family, your company, and, significantly, the well-being of your society at large. My experience has consistently reinforced this belief: when a leader openly demonstrates genuine, heartfelt caring for these facets, it is not just commendable; it is transformative. Such a leader, who embraces and embodies this profound level of caring in an authentic and natural manner, is destined for unparalleled success. Their leadership becomes more than a role; it evolves into a beacon of inspiration and a catalyst for positive change.

A multitude of texts and studies conclude that various traits underpin the archetype of natural leaders, traits like self-awareness, communication skills, empathy and compassion, adaptability, ethical and moral integrity, continuous learning and development, relationship building, motivation and inspiration, and strategic vision. My repeated interjection of care alongside each characteristic is no error.

Let us delve into each trait:

- **Self-awareness** can be viewed as a form of care turned inward, a reflection on one's own abilities and impact on others.

- **Communication skills** represent care in articulation, ensuring clarity and understanding in interactions.
- **Empathy and compassion** are perhaps the most direct expressions of care, meaning a leader's ability to connect with the emotions and well-being of others.
- **Adaptability** showcases care in response to change, maintaining steadiness amid flux.
- **Ethical and moral integrity** demonstrate care for societal norms and greater good, a compass that guides actions and decisions.
- **Continuous learning and development** embody care in personal growth and the evolution of one's leadership capabilities.
- **Building relationships** is essentially about nurturing care in the social fabric of an organization.
- **Motivation and inspiration** reveal care for driving teams towards common goals with zeal and enthusiasm.
- **Strategic vision** is care projected into the future, a roadmap for the prosperity and success of the collective.

Care is a fundamental part of leadership, intertwined with every quality that defines a true leader. Let us analyze them a bit deeper one by one:

Self-awareness
Caring about personal growth and self-improvement leads to self-awareness and a better understanding of one's leadership style. Richard Branson, the founder of the Virgin Group, is a prime example of this philosophy. He is known for his dedication to continuous self-improvement and his openness to feedback. Branson's approach to leadership is grounded in self-awareness,

which he uses not only to enhance his own skills but also to inspire others around him. His commitment to personal growth and his willingness to learn from both successes and failures demonstrate the importance of self-improvement in effective leadership. Branson's journey reflects the idea that caring about one's own development is a key component of setting a positive example for others to follow.

Communication skills

Caring about conveying clear, honest, and motivational messages enhances effective communication. This is about ensuring that people on the other side are clear, motivated, and inspired and that dialogue is open for the success of both parties. Steve Jobs' ability to articulate a vision and inspire his team reflects an excellent example of his caring about his company, organization, and customers.

Empathy and compassion

Fostering empathy and compassion comes down to caring for the well-being of team members, customers, or family members. Care is at the core, as exemplified by Howard Schultz of Starbucks, who created comprehensive health benefits for employees, demonstrating his genuine concern for their well-being.

Adaptability

Care for the team and project success fosters adaptability and a willingness to change. This adaptability is a direct result of the underlying care. A prime example of this is Reed Hastings' strategic shift of Netflix from DVD rentals to streaming. This adaptation was in response to evolving consumer preferences. It demonstrates his commitment to business continuity, which not only helped retain existing jobs within the company but also created new job opportunities worldwide.

Ethical and moral integrity
Having a deep concern for acting correctly forms the foundation of ethical and moral integrity. Once again, care is the fundamental element! This principle is exemplified by the legendary investor Warren Buffet's commitment to ethical business practices. His actions clearly show his dedication to doing what is right.

Continuous learning and development
Prioritizing both personal and professional growth fuels a culture of continuous learning and development. Satya Nadella's leadership at Microsoft, which is centered on learning and growth, reflects this principle. It showcases care for personal development (not ego-driven, but genuine care), for the company's members, and for society as a whole.

Building relationships
Caring about meaningful relationships fosters a supportive and collaborative environment. A great example is Richard Branson's emphasis on employee relationships and creating a family-like atmosphere at Virgin.

Motivation and inspiration
Caring about the goals and aspirations of the team, family, corporation, or country drives motivation and inspiration. Elon Musk's vision-driven leadership at SpaceX and Tesla motivates teams toward ambitious goals. Elon Musk is said to be not an easy leader or manager, so why does he have so many loyal coworkers, partners, and employees? Because he shows he cares.

Strategic vision
Caring about the long-term success of the organization guides strategic vision. Jeff Bezos' long-term vision for Amazon demonstrates caring about sustainable success.

Nelson Mandela exhibited care through his dedication to fighting apartheid in South Africa, which showcased his concern for the rights and dignity of all people in his country, regardless of their race. His ability to forgive and work with those who had oppressed him and his followers demonstrated a level of care and understanding that was revolutionary. That is how he led hundreds of thousands of people. While this demonstrates care versus leadership, in this book, we will demonstrate care, especially in leading a group of unknown individuals toward corporate or business goals.

In the corporate world, leaders of Disney have always impressed me with how they showed care for their teams around the world. They encourage their leaders to establish positive norms, offer training opportunities, and align the organization's mission with daily realities, which is a method to show care for the personal and professional development of their team members, which in return incarnates itself for care for our most beloved ones: our children. These care strategies foster a positive work environment that, in turn, can enhance employee satisfaction, engagement, and productivity, aligning with Disney's long-standing success in its industry.

I trust that my insights have highlighted a fundamental trait shared by all great leaders: caring. This element, in its various forms and expressions, is central to effective leadership, and it is most impactful when demonstrated genuinely and naturally.

In later sections of the book, we will showcase activities centered around care that have been instrumental in the success of the remote and gig-freelancer communities with which I have been working.

"It is not the strongest of the species that survive, nor the most intelligent, but the one most responsive to change."
Charles Darwin

Navigating New Horizons: Leadership in the Remote and Gig Economy Era

The World Health Organization (WHO) declared the COVID-19 pandemic on March 11, 2020.

The pandemic has been widely cited as a transformative event, profoundly impacting numerous aspects of our lives across the globe. It has not only reshaped our daily routines and personal interactions but has also brought about sweeping changes in the business landscape and altered our collective outlook on life. This pandemic, a topic of numerous discussions and analyses, serves as a critical reference point for understanding how a global crisis can redefine norms and expectations in both personal and professional aspects in many countries around the world.

The shift to remote work driven by the pandemic has been like setting sail into uncharted waters for numerous traditional companies. This transition was not just about relocating work from offices to homes. It represented a profound transformation in how businesses operate, interact, and grow. Companies, many steeped in conventional in-office cultures, suddenly found themselves in a whirlwind of change, bringing in a plethora of new employees from diverse locations and time zones. This virtual expansion of the workforce presented unique challenges in onboarding and fostering engagement through screens and digital tools. This paradigm shift was more than a logistical challenge; it was a solid test for leadership. The art of leadership, often thought of in the context of physical office spaces where daily interactions and in-person meetings were the norms, faced its tough test. Leaders who were once adept at navigating the familiar corridors of their offices and engaging with teams face-to-face found themselves at a crossroads. The virtual environment exposed a stark reality: leading a remote team demanded more than just traditional management skills; it required adaptability, empathy, and an innovative mindset.

The office, once a common ground and a physical manifestation of a company's culture and ethos, was replaced by digital workspaces. The familiar rhythm of office life, the impromptu conversations by the water cooler, and the non-verbal cues in meeting rooms were all suddenly absent. Leaders had to reimagine their approach, learning to connect, inspire, and guide their teams across digital divides. The change was not just about adapting to technology; it was about redefining leadership in a landscape where physical presence was no longer a given.

For many, this was a journey from familiar shores to the deep and often turbulent seas of remote work. It demanded a reevaluation of leadership styles, communication strategies, and team dynamics. The leaders who thrived were those who saw this as an opportunity to innovate and grow, understanding that effective leadership in a remote world is not just about managing tasks but about nurturing relationships, building trust, and fostering a sense of community, even from afar.

In these times where remote roles and gig economies are becoming the norm, the nature of leadership is undergoing a profound transformation. At the heart of this change is the recognition that while leadership skills can be developed and refined, the most critical component of effective leadership, which is care, must be an inherent part of one's character. This understanding is crucial as organizations navigate the future of work, characterized by its remote nature and the unknown workforce that comes with gig and freelance arrangements.

The future of work demands a unique breed of leaders, ones who possess an innate capacity for empathy and care. This fundamental quality, deeply embedded in their DNA, is what sets them apart. It is not merely about having the ability to strategize or execute; it is about possessing a natural predisposition toward understanding and empathizing with others. While skills like decision-making, communication, and organizational expertise are essential and can be nurtured, the core attribute of care is irreplaceable and non-negotiable. It is like a seed of potential that some are born with, which can be cultivated but not implanted where it does not exist yet.

As we look towards the future, companies, groups, and organizations face the critical task of identifying and nurturing this talent. In a landscape dominated by remote interactions and a gig workforce, the challenge lies in finding leaders who not only have the foundational skill of care but also the ability to effectively lead a diverse and dispersed team. The leaders who will thrive in this new environment are those who can connect with their team members beyond the constraints of physical proximity, building trust and fostering a sense of community and belonging, even from a distance. This requirement places a significant emphasis on the recruitment and development processes within organizations. The task is no longer just about evaluating a candidate's resume or professional accomplishments; it is about discerning their inherent capacity for empathy and care. In this context, leadership recruitment transforms into a more holistic and intuitive process, where understanding a candidate's core character traits becomes as important as assessing their professional skills.

The leaders best suited for this new era are those who inherently understand and value the importance of care in their leadership approach. While many aspects of leadership can be developed over time, the ability to lead with empathy and care is a natural trait that must exist at the core of a leader's persona. Organizations must prioritize this intrinsic quality when selecting leaders, as it is the bedrock upon which successful remote or gig workforce management is built. Adopting this leadership approach promises not only to drive impressive business outcomes but also to foster a more cohesive, engaged, and content workforce.

It is pretty interesting to observe the myriad of articles, books, and resources offering guidance on effective leadership. These materials can undoubtedly provide valuable insights and, help develop good managerial skills and help natural-born leaders to develop those qualities. However, when it comes to the quintessence of leadership, particularly the essential aspect of care, I hold a somewhat skeptical view of the notion that great leaders can be entirely **made**. While these resources are beneficial for shaping competent managers, there is a distinct difference between a good manager and a leader who can achieve exceptional results, especially in environments where team members are remote and may not have direct personal connections with their leaders. In such settings, the intrinsic ability to care and connect deeply with one's team becomes even more critical. This quality, I believe, is not something that can be fully instilled through external resources; it is a fundamental trait that great leaders must possess at their core.

Now, let's examine the data that underscores the necessity for exceptional leadership over excellent management. This analysis is rooted in our fundamental element, care, and takes into account the emerging trends in the future of work.

- In his article "Freelance Market Statistics & Trends[14]," Varun Omprakash analyses the freelance market statistics and trends in the United States, and he states freelancing is anticipated to continue growing in the United States, with over 1.4 trillion US$ contributed to the economy. The steady increase in individuals opting for freelancing is expected to make freelancers the majority of the workforce in the United States soon.
- According to TeamStage, the global gig economy generates 204 billion US$ in gross volume and is expected to grow to around 455 billion US$ by 2023[15]
- An article "405 Freelance Statistics for 2023: Market Size, Profile Data & Salary Rates" in financesonline[16] states that the gig economy accounts for up to 12% of the labor market worldwide, referencing the World Bank as its source of information.

What is impressive is to see that freelancing is more common among younger generations, with 43% of Gen Z and 46% of millennial professionals in the United States workforce being freelancers, compared to 35% of Gen X and 27% of baby boomers[17]. Freelancing also attracts more educated workers, with 26% of all United States. freelancers holding a postgraduate degree, an increase from 20% in 2021. As you can clearly see, the world is going towards a work-life-balance-based, environmentally friendly, and free-choice work and economy, which is based on gig and freelancing. Additionally, many companies are adopting hybrid or remote work as alternatives to the traditional brick-and-mortar models or companies that have their workforce under the same roof every single day.

I have been working with thousands of freelancers during my corporate roles, of which more than six years in a multi-billion US$ company, and believe it or not, a properly led set of freelancers will deliver excellent outcomes not only in jobs to be done but also in terms of social good and community. This can be achieved only through leadership that is, in essence, based on care. Then again comes the question: how come thousands of people, in this case, gig-freelancers working on behalf of an organization within a corporation, can deliver significantly better results than full-time employees executing the same jobs, working day in and day out under the same roof?

Moreover, I have observed organizations with a structure mirroring my own in managing remote workers yet yielding decidedly unfavorable results. This clearly indicates that success is not rooted in the structure itself but rather in the presence of effective leadership. Is this a result of some mystical force? Certainly not. The key lies in the presence of leaders who genuinely **care**.

Over the past 35 years of my career, I have passionately dedicated myself to transforming teams. These teams, initially disengaged, disconnected, and unclear about their roles in the grand scheme, often produced costly and subpar results. My mission has been to convert them into high-performing units that not only excel in their tasks but also care deeply about their work, each other, and their social impact. A significant portion of this transformational journey involved remote teams, with many team members that I have never met in person. The most profound lesson from my extensive experience is this: success, exceptional outcomes, and extraordinary collaboration are achievable regardless of the team's background, beliefs, or location. The key lies in focusing on caring and demonstrating this quality through actions. This approach has been central to my success in nurturing high-performing teams.

Let us consider the dynamics of manager-worker relationships. With an average or great manager, the connection often dissipates once either party moves on. Reflect for a moment: How often do you reach out to your former managers unless there was a personal bond? Conversely, think about the leaders who showed genuine care. How often do you find yourself reaching out to them? This distinction might seem subtle, yet it is profound. Great managers can coach you to excel in your role or assist in finding a new job. But a great leader who shows care does something far more impactful: they inspire and motivate you to achieve life goals that resonate with your soul, and this makes the biggest difference.

"The greatest leader is not necessarily the one who does the greatest things. He is the one that gets the people to do the greatest things."
Ronald Reagan

The Alchemy of Leadership: Transforming Team Dynamics

Let's embark on an enlightening exploration into a captivating aspect of leadership dynamics. This journey will take us deep into understanding how the quality and nature of leadership can drastically shape and redefine the performance and morale of a team.

Picture a situation where a group of people, maybe struggling with a certain kind of boss, suddenly starts doing well and growing when a new, caring leader takes charge. In stark contrast, we will also investigate situations where teams that once thrived, achieving remarkable success and cohesion, begin to unravel and lose their luster when new, less empathetic leadership takes the helm. The examples in this section aim to unravel the threads of what makes leadership truly effective and transformative. It is proof of the fact that leadership transcends the conventional boundaries of management. It is not merely about delegating tasks, meeting targets, or maintaining order. Instead, it delves into the deeper domains of human connection, understanding, and empathy. In the examples we will discuss, you will witness the almost alchemical change that occurs when a leader who genuinely cares and connects with their team steps in.

Leadership, in its most impactful form, is about creating an environment where individuals feel valued, understood, and inspired. It is about building a culture where the collective goals of the team are pursued by the people with passion and dedication, not because they have to, but because they want to. This shift in approach can be the difference between a team that merely functions and one that excels.

We will explore how caring leadership does not mean a lack of rigor or high standards. Instead, it signifies a balance where expectations and achievements are pursued with a compassionate understanding of each team member's unique strengths and challenges. This balance is crucial, especially in remote or gig work environments, where physical distance can often lead to a sense of disconnection and isolation. A caring leader bridges this gap, creating a sense of belonging and community, irrespective of geographical boundaries. On the flip side, the other examples will demonstrate how a change in leadership to a more transactional, less caring approach can have detrimental effects. Teams that once worked harmoniously can become disjointed, and their sense of purpose and motivation diminished. This decline is often rapid and palpable, leading to a decrease in productivity, a drop in morale, and, in some cases, a complete disintegration of what was once a thriving team dynamic.

My aim is to illuminate the lasting mark that a leader's approach can leave on their team. The stories shared will not only provide insights into the mechanics of effective leadership but also inspire current and aspiring leaders. They will serve as a clear indication that the heart of outstanding leadership lies in the ability to care genuinely and lead with empathy, particularly in today's evolving work landscape of remote or gig-based teams. It is a call to embrace a leadership style that values and uplifts people, recognizing that the true measure of a leader's success is reflected in the growth, satisfaction, and achievements of their team.

The resurgence of Apple Inc.
In the late 1990s, Apple Inc. was on the verge of bankruptcy. The situation was so dire that it was hard to see a way out. However, in 1997, Steve Jobs, one of the co-founders, returned as the CEO. Jobs was not just a visionary; he cared deeply about Apple and its mission to create user-friendly, aesthetically pleasing tech products. He was a great communicator who cared that his organization also cared. His infamous attention to detail stemmed from a genuine concern for delivering quality to the customers, an extension of his caring attitude. He led the team to innovate relentlessly, resulting in groundbreaking products like the iMac, iPhone, and iPad. Under his caring yet demanding leadership, Apple did not just recover; it soared to become one of the most valuable companies globally. His leadership exemplified how a caring attitude towards both the product and the team can lead to extraordinary achievements.

Marvel's heroic comeback
Marvel Entertainment was facing bankruptcy in the late 1990s. The future looked bleak until Isaac Perlmutter stepped in with a vision and a caring approach towards the brand's legacy and the creative talent it housed. Perlmutter understood the potential of Marvel's vast array of characters and the emotional connection they had with the audience. He nurtured a culture of creativity and collaboration, leading to the origin of the Marvel Cinematic Universe. Under his leadership, Marvel did not just recover from bankruptcy; it emerged as a cultural phenomenon, showcasing that caring leadership combined with innovative thinking can lead to legendary turnarounds.

Chipotle Mexican grill

This one might not be so well known; however, personally, it is the one that inspires me most. Chipotle was a successful fast-food chain that offered fresh and healthy ingredients to its customers. It had a loyal fan base and a strong reputation. But everything changed in 2015 when a series of food safety scandals hit the company. Customers got sick from eating contaminated food, and the media reported on the incidents. Chipotle's sales and stock price plummeted, and its brand image was tarnished.

The company's founder and CEO, Steve Ells, built Chipotle from scratch, and he was proud of his vision and values. He believed that he knew what was best for the company, and he resisted any suggestions or changes from others. He tried to fix the problems by implementing new protocols and procedures, but they were not enough. He failed to communicate effectively with his employees, customers, and stakeholders. He also failed to show empathy and care for those who were affected by the crisis.

The situation got worse in 2016 when another outbreak of foodborne illness occurred. The public lost trust in Chipotle, and many people stopped eating there. The company faced lawsuits, investigations, and regulatory pressures. Ells realized that he could not handle the crisis alone, and he decided to step down as CEO. He announced that he was looking for a successor who could lead Chipotle to a new era.

In 2018, Brian Niccol was appointed as the new CEO of Chipotle. He had previously led Taco Bell, another fast-food chain that had undergone a successful transformation. Niccol brought a new vision and culture (of caring) to Chipotle. He focused on improving food quality, enhancing digital capabilities, expanding menu options, and launching marketing campaigns. He also focused on caring for his employees, customers, and communities. He listened to their feedback, addressed their concerns, and rewarded their loyalty. He showed them that he genuinely cared about their health, happiness, and satisfaction. Under Niccol's leadership, Chipotle recovered from its crisis and achieved record sales and profits. It regained its popularity and reputation and attracted new customers and investors. It also became a leader in social responsibility and environmental sustainability. It donated millions of dollars to various causes, such as education, health care, and disaster relief. It also reduced its carbon footprint and waste production and increased its use of organic and local ingredients.

Chipotle's story shows that a great leader makes a difference. A great leader is not only visionary and innovative but also caring and empathetic. A great leader cares about the people who work with him, the people who buy from him, and the people who live around him. A great leader cares about making a positive impact on the world.

Chicago Bulls

The Chicago Bulls was a struggling basketball team in the late 1980s. They had some talented players, such as Michael Jordan and Scottie Pippen, but they could not pass their rivals, the Detroit Pistons, who were known for their physical and aggressive style of play. The Bulls were frustrated and demoralized, and they needed a change. In 1989, the Bulls hired Phil Jackson as their new head coach. Jackson was a former player who had won two championships with the New York Knicks in the 1970s. He had a different approach to coaching than his predecessors. He introduced a system called the "triangle offense," which emphasized ball movement, spacing, and teamwork. He also used a philosophy called "Zen," which involved meditation, mindfulness, and self-awareness. He taught his players how to cope with stress, anger, and ego and how to focus on the present moment. Jackson cared about his players as individuals, not only as athletes. He learned about their backgrounds, personalities, and interests. He gave them books to read, movies to watch, and music to listen to. He challenged them to grow and improve, not only on the court but also in their personal lives. He respected their opinions and encouraged them to express themselves. He also cared about their health and well-being and gave them rest and recovery time when needed. Under Jackson's leadership, the Bulls transformed from a frustrated and divided team to a confident and united one. They developed a strong chemistry and trust among themselves, and they played with joy and passion. They overcame their nemesis, the Pistons, and went on to win six championships in eight years. They became one of the greatest teams in NBA history, and Jackson became one of the greatest coaches of all time.

The Bulls' story shows that a great leader makes a difference. A great leader cares about the people who work with him, the people who support him, and the people who compete against him. Same team, different leader with a naturally exposed caring attitude and approach, and outstanding outcomes.

Now, let's shift our attention to some real examples where a highly successful company begins to falter under the leadership of managers who fail to adhere to genuine leadership principles. We can find organizations and teams that were outperforming in every aspect thanks to a genuinely caring leader, and once the leader left and the group of people or organization started to be led by non-caring leaders, things went down the drain.

The fall of Starbucks
Starbucks is one of the most successful coffee chains in the world, with over 30,000 stores in 80 countries. The company was founded by Howard Schultz, who had a vision of creating a "third place" between home and work, where people could enjoy quality coffee and connect with each other. Schultz was a caring leader who valued his employees, whom he called "partners," and offered them generous benefits, such as health insurance, stock options, and tuition reimbursement. He also cared about his customers, whom he considered "guests," and invested in creating a warm and welcoming atmosphere in his stores. He also cared about his community and supported various social causes, such as

environmental sustainability, fair trade, and diversity. The most important thing is that with every action he took and every word he said, he exposed his genuine care for everything that surrounded him, and that was a fundamental difference.

However, in 2000, Schultz decided to step down as CEO and become chairman of the board. He was replaced by Jim Donald, who had a different approach to leadership. Donald focused on expanding the company's growth and profitability and neglected the core values that Schultz had established. He cut costs by reducing the quality of the coffee beans, introducing automated espresso machines, and adding more products to the menu, such as breakfast sandwiches and CDs. He also reduced the training and development of the employees and increased their workload and pressure. He alienated the customers by making the stores more standardized and impersonal and losing the distinctive aroma and flavor of Starbucks coffee.

As a result of Donald's leadership, Starbucks lost its competitive edge and its loyal fan base. The company's sales and stock price declined, and it faced increasing competition from other chains, such as Dunkin' Donuts and McDonald's. It took several years for Starbucks to recover from the damage done by Donald's leadership.

The decline of Apple
Apple is one of the most innovative and influential technology companies in the world, with iconic products such as the Macintosh, the iPod, the iPhone, and the iPad. The company was co-founded by Steve Jobs, a visionary leader with a passion for design and creativity. Jobs was a caring leader who inspired his employees to pursue excellence and challenge the status quo. He also cared about his customers, whom he called "the crazy ones," and delivered products that met their needs and desires. He also cared about his industry and revolutionized several fields, such as personal computing, music, mobile phones, and tablets.

However, in 1985, Jobs was forced out of Apple by John Sculley, who was hired as CEO by Jobs himself. Sculley had a different vision for Apple than Jobs. Sculley focused on increasing the company's market share and profitability and neglected the core values that Jobs had established. He increased the product line by introducing many variations of the Macintosh, which confused the customers and diluted the brand identity. He also reduced the research and development budget and ignored the emerging trends in technology, such as graphical user interfaces, networking, and multimedia. As a result of Sculley's leadership, Apple lost its competitive advantage and its loyal customer base. The company's sales and stock prices plummeted, and they faced increasing competition from other technology companies, such as Microsoft, IBM, Dell, and Compaq.

In 1997, Jobs returned as CEO after Apple acquired NeXT Computer Inc., which he founded after leaving Apple. He tried to restore the company by simplifying the product line, reinventing the Macintosh with the iMac, introducing new products such as the iPod, iPhone, and iPad, and rebranding Apple as a lifestyle company. It took several years for Apple to regain its position as one of the most valuable companies in the world.

You can see it might take years, and if ever possible, to recover an organization or team from a disaster built by an uncaring leader. This means losing market share, losing trust, losing customers, and losing reputation. Building a reputation is a challenging and long road; destroying it is easy and fast.

The demise of Enron

Enron was one of the largest energy companies in the world, with operations in over 30 countries. The company was led by Kenneth Lay, who was a charismatic leader with a vision of transforming Enron into a global leader in energy trading and diversifying into new markets, such as broadband, water, and power plants. Lay was a caring leader who empowered his employees to take risks and rewarded them with generous bonuses and stock options. He also cared about his shareholders, whom he considered "the owners," and delivered consistent growth and high returns. He also cared about his community and supported various charitable causes, such as education, health, and arts.

However, in 2001, Lay resigned as CEO and was replaced by Jeffrey Skilling, who had a different style of leadership than Lay. Skilling focused on maximizing the company's earnings and stock price and neglected the core values that Lay had established. He created a culture of greed and deception, where employees were encouraged to manipulate the financial statements, hide the losses, and inflate the profits. He also exploited the loopholes in the accounting and regulatory systems and engaged in fraudulent and illegal activities, such as insider trading, market manipulation, and tax evasion. As a result of Skilling's leadership, Enron collapsed into bankruptcy and scandal. The company's revenues and stock prices plunged to zero, and it faced numerous investigations and lawsuits from the government, the regulators, the creditors, and the shareholders. Thousands of employees lost their jobs and their retirement savings, which were tied to Enron's stock. Thousands of customers and suppliers were affected by Enron's failure. The company's reputation and trust were destroyed.

Here is the essence of my argument: yes, one can acquire knowledge in management, processes, law, finance, technology, operations, and manufacturing. These are skills that can be learned, honed, and mastered. However, when it comes to the genuine, heartfelt capacity to care, truly care, I firmly believe that this is not something that can be taught or learned. It is an innate quality, something you are either born with or without, and the examples I shared clearly illustrate this. Despite the plethora of bestselling leadership books, despite the numerous expensive courses with their flashy marketing, and regardless of the well-intentioned advice from mentors and trusted sources, the ability to authentically care, and to express this care through actions and words, is intrinsic. It is either a part of who you are, or it is not. It is that simple. This intrinsic nature of genuine caring is precisely why truly great leaders are a rarity, particularly those who can effectively lead the unknown workforce, the remote teams, the gig workers, and the freelancers who are often just names on a screen. When we do encounter an exceptional leader who successfully guides these unknown teams to remarkable success, it is awe-inspiring. We often find ourselves searching for the secret formula. Could it really be something superficial, like the cool black T-shirt they wear, paired with jeans and comfortable sports shoes?

But the truth lies deeper. It is about that innate ability to care and connect, transcending the physical and conventional barriers of traditional leadership. This is the kind of leadership that leaves a lasting impact, creating a ripple effect of inspiration and motivation. As we ponder the rarity of such leaders, it is worth reflecting on the essence of what makes them stand out. It is not about the attire, the charisma, or even the eloquence – it is about the genuine care that resonates in every action and decision they make. This is the kind of leadership that does not just manage teams but transforms them, creating a legacy of inspiration and achievement.

"Leadership is not about titles, positions, or flowcharts. It is about one life influencing another."
John C. Maxwell

Leading Local Known Teams vs Remote Unknown Teams

In my extensive career spanning over three and a half decades, predominantly in the IT sector across major corporations in Europe and the US, I have had the enriching experience of leading both local and remote teams. This journey has offered me a broad spectrum of insights, particularly in understanding the dynamics of leadership versus management.

When it comes to leading a local team, the advantages are many, especially if one naturally inclines towards a caring leadership style. However, even in these seemingly advantageous settings, I have witnessed numerous managers (and I deliberately use the term "managers," not "leaders") grappling with the challenges of effectively leading their teams. Often, these managers are products of management assessment programs. In my observation, these programs frequently miss the mark. They seem to prioritize competencies that are, at best, superficial, easily mimicked by anyone with a talent for acting the part. The real test, however, comes with employee satisfaction surveys or what many refer to as employee polls. These are the moments when the shortcomings of such selections become glaringly evident.

The crux of the issue lies in the inability of these programs to truly gauge a candidate's natural inclination towards caring – an essential trait for genuine leadership. It is a simple truth: you cannot fake leadership indefinitely. A mask of leadership, devoid of authentic care and empathy, is unsustainable. When teams perceive this lack of genuine leadership, their engagement and motivation inevitably drop. The result is a sterile management that fails to resonate with my core belief: the power of genuine caring. This disconnect not only impacts overall outcomes but also leads to higher turnover rates. The saying "people don't leave jobs, they leave managers" rings particularly true in these scenarios.

While I do not claim to be an exceptional leader, the teams I have led have consistently demonstrated significant progress in both engagement and performance. This, I believe, is proof of the impact of leadership style. The same team under different leaderships can yield vastly different results. This phenomenon likely resonates with many.

Now, let's look into the contrasting challenges of leading a local team, where you have the opportunity for physical and mental connections, versus managing remote teams, especially those comprising gig workers or freelancers. The latter often presents a unique set of challenges, given their transient nature and the lack of personal interaction. Interestingly, in my experience, some of the most effective leaders I have encountered were those who managed remotely. We never met in person, yet their leadership surpassed that of many local managers, whom I hesitate to label as leaders. This experience has led me to a profound realization: effective leadership transcends physical boundaries. It is not the proximity that defines a leader's effectiveness but their ability to foster a sense of connection, purpose, and motivation, irrespective of geographical distances.

Whether leading local teams or navigating the complexities of remote team management, the underlying principle remains unchanged: genuine caring and the ability to inspire and connect deeply with team members are the hallmarks of authentic leadership. This principle has been a guiding light in my career, shaping my approach to leading diverse teams in various settings.

To fully explore the complexities and nuances of managing or leading a remote team, distinct from the dynamics of a gig-freelancing ensemble, let's deep dive into the six most relevant aspects, which are communication, performance management, team cohesion, work-life balance, trust building, and adaptability, each revealing different facets of the challenges inherent in remote leadership. This exploration will help us uncover the intricate layers and sometimes hidden obstacles that come with steering a team separated by distance yet united in purpose.

Communication

Communication emerges as a central and transformative component, significantly shaping relationships, trust, and understanding within a team. It is "the" most important aspect of human relationships. In leading remote or gig-freelancer teams, we enter a domain where the dynamics of interaction are fundamentally altered by the absence of a shared physical environment, introducing both unique challenges and opportunities. Setting out on the path of full-time remote work, I was met with a unique series of challenges that are a signature of this digital era. Among these was the difficulty of interpreting non-verbal cues from workers, colleagues and leaders, an aspect that, in a conventional office setting, plays a crucial role in understanding underlying sentiments and intentions. This lack of physical presence often led me down a path of making assumptions, which can often be tinged with a negative bias.

I recall a particularly telling incident that unfolded in this context. Following a heated debate with my manager, there was a noticeable shift in our interactions. The weekly one-on-one meetings, which had been a cornerstone of our communication, began to be canceled sporadically. Given the timing, right after an intense discussion and amidst the broader organizational struggles, I could not help but draw a direct connection between the two events. I started to believe that these cancellations were a repercussion of our disagreement and thoughts like "my manager no longer values my contributions" began to cloud my judgment. However, the reality, as I later discovered, was far from what I had imagined. After persistently reaching out through Microsoft Teams, I finally got the opportunity to address my concerns directly with my manager. To my surprise, his explanation painted a completely different picture. He highlighted that the organization was indeed facing challenges, but my department was functioning effectively. His focus had shifted to areas that required more immediate attention, which led to the temporary suspension of our meetings.

This experience was a profound learning moment, underscoring several key insights:

The danger of assumptions
In remote work environments, it is easy to misinterpret situations when we do not have access to all the information. What we perceive as reality is often a reflection of our own biases and fears.

The importance of timely clarification
Instead of allowing misconceptions to fester and cause unnecessary stress, it is crucial to seek clarity. This proactive approach not only alleviates personal anxiety but also fosters open and honest communication.

The critical role of communication in remote teams

Effective communication is the lifeline of remote work. It ensures that everyone is aligned and prevents misunderstandings that can arise from the lack of face-to-face interactions.

This incident taught me that in the remote working world, clear and direct communication is more than just a tool; it is an essential strategy for navigating the complexities of digital interactions. It reminds us that while technology has enabled us to work across boundaries, the fundamental principles of human interaction, which are understanding, clarity, and empathy, remain as vital as ever.

In local teams, the ease of reading non-verbal cues and emotions facilitates a more immediate and engaging form of communication. Proximity allows for real-time clarification of doubts and the sharing of ideas, bolstered by the informal, yet significant, exchanges that occur in shared physical spaces like coffee breaks and corridor talks.

Conversely, remote teams navigate a different terrain. Heavily reliant on digital communication tools, they face the challenges of bridging time zones, cultures, and virtual platforms. The establishment of trust, rapport, and team cohesion becomes more complex in this environment, often exacerbated by delayed feedback and the potential for messages to be misinterpreted or felt impersonal. Furthermore, the multitude of digital channels can lead to communication overload, diluting the clarity and impact of leadership signals.

These theoretical frameworks find reflection in real-life examples. In a local team setting, a manager might engage in regular, direct interactions with team members, providing immediate feedback and acknowledging their achievements. In contrast, a remote team leader must adeptly utilize various communication tools to maintain connection and address the concerns of their team while also celebrating successes in a dispersed work environment.

Local team:
- Easier to read non-verbal cues and emotions.
- Immediate mutual feedback.
- Can be more personal and engaging.
- Team members can easily clarify doubts or discuss ideas in real time.
- Coffee and corridor talks help a lot.

Remote team:
- Relies heavily on digital communication tools.
- Harder to communicate across time zones, cultures, and platforms.
- More challenges in establishing trust, rapport, and cohesion.
- Delayed feedback.
- Risk of misinterpretation or feeling impersonal.
- Potential for communication overload with numerous digital channels.
- Leadership signals risk being diluted.

A study by VitalSmarts[18] found that 52% of remote workers felt that their colleagues did not treat them equally, and 41% felt that their colleagues said bad things behind their backs. Difficult to deal with, isn't it? But a caring leader can drive the right culture to overcome those undesired circumstances, directly or indirectly.

A survey by Buffer[19] found that 20% of remote workers struggled with loneliness and 20% with communication. A naturally empathetic leader is essential in addressing the isolation felt by remote workers. It is less about frequent calls and more about recognizing the problem and cultivating a nurturing environment within the team or the entire organization.

Performance management
Performance management, a critical aspect of leading teams, takes on distinct characteristics when comparing local teams to remote

or gig-freelancer teams. This section delves into these differences on a high level, unraveling the complexities and nuances associated with evaluating and guiding team performance in varied work environments.

In local teams, the proximity of team members allows for a more straightforward observation of performance and provision of real-time feedback. This closeness fosters a sense of consistency and fairness in performance appraisal and reward systems. Issues can be addressed promptly, and there is generally more clarity and alignment of performance goals and expectations. The physical presence of team members and their immediate environment offers a tangible context for assessing performance and ensuring that the goals are well understood and pursued effectively.

On the contrary, remote teams, which include gig-freelancers, often operate under a performance management paradigm that is markedly different. Here, the metrics for assessing performance may lean more toward results-oriented approaches. The lack of physical proximity can lead to potential delays in addressing issues, less consistency, and perceived fairness in appraisals and rewards. Moreover, remote settings might witness less clarity and alignment on performance goals and expectations. Consequently, there is an increased need for trust and autonomy in the management of performance, making it crucial for leaders to adapt their strategies to these unique challenges.

Throughout my career, I have experienced the contrasting dynamics of working onsite, near my management team and peers, and the distinct challenges of remote work. Regardless of my work setting, I have consistently taken the initiative to proactively seek feedback from my managers. This proactive approach was particularly crucial when working with managers who were less adept at communication, especially in a remote context. One striking observation from these experiences was the apparent disparity in interaction and recognition between team members who were physically close to the management and those who, like me, worked remotely. In the world of performance management, where employees are often ranked, I noticed a trend: colleagues who shared a physical workspace with the manager frequently seemed to receive swifter promotions and greater acknowledgment despite my efforts to demonstrate superior performance through clear key performance indicators (KPIs) and outcomes. However, this was not a universal rule and varied significantly depending on the leader or manager in question. Some leaders were adept at separating casual, in-person interactions, like coffee chats and happy hour gatherings, from the formalities of performance management. They could recognize and reward performance irrespective of the employee's physical location. Yet, even with such equitable leaders, a shadow of doubt lingered in my mind. This experience taught me an important lesson: the necessity of being exceptionally proactive in seeking feedback. In a remote work environment, where physical cues and informal conversations are absent, regular and explicit communication about one's performance becomes vital. It is crucial to seek out and engage in frequent, direct discussions about performance to avoid unexpected revelations during formal reviews.

The underlying message here is clear: In the new world of work, the traditional metrics and methods of performance assessment need to be adapted. As an employee, taking charge of your own performance narrative by regularly soliciting feedback, presenting your achievements, and advocating for your progress is essential. This approach not only helps in aligning perceptions with reality but also bridges the gap that physical distance can create in the workplace.

Local team managers conducting regular performance reviews with transparent criteria and offering direct feedback and recognition find themselves on a different playing field compared to leaders managing a remote team. In the remote context, performance check-ins might be less frequent, criteria more adaptive, and the emphasis shifts toward coaching and support. The effectiveness of such approaches hinges on how well they are executed and integrated into the broader organizational culture.

Local team:
- Easier to observe performance and provide real-time feedback.
- More consistency and fairness in performance appraisal and reward systems.
- Can address issues promptly.
- More clarity and alignment on performance goals and expectations.

Remote team:
- Performance metrics may be more results-oriented.
- Potential delay in addressing issues.
- Less consistency and fairness in performance appraisal and reward systems.
- Less clarity and alignment on performance goals and expectations.
- More need for trust and autonomy in performance management.

A Gallup study[20] explores performance management strategies suitable for remote and hybrid teams. It identifies two performance domains critical for success in a role: setting goals and meeting them. The study suggests that establishing clear goals and measuring performance against them is crucial for managing remote and hybrid teams effectively.

A truly exceptional leader, even when guiding remote or gig-freelancer teams, has the unique capability to inspire and motivate their team to not only achieve but exceed their goals. This leader understands the importance of providing relevant and meaningful information that resonates with each team member. They are consistently available for any issues or support their team might need, effectively bridging the distance inherent in remote work. Furthermore, they are adept at implementing tools and systems that offer timely and constructive feedback on performance. This approach ensures that the team not only meets its objectives but also feels empowered and valued, leading to extraordinary results.

Team cohesion

The concept of team cohesion, vital for any successful team, assumes different forms and challenges when comparing local teams with remote or gig-freelancer teams.

In local teams, there are inherent advantages that naturally foster team cohesion. The physical proximity of team members creates abundant opportunities for bonding, making it easier to build shared culture, values, and norms. This environment tends to nurture trust, commitment, and satisfaction among team members, positively impacting their social support and emotional well-being. The shared identity that evolves in such settings is often a product of daily interactions, common experiences, and the unspoken understanding that develops in a shared physical space.

Contrast this with remote teams, where the quest for team cohesion demands a more deliberate and strategic effort. The absence of physical proximity and shared daily experiences can lead to a sense of isolation and a lack of a common culture. Building team cohesion based on shared identity, values, and norms becomes a more challenging endeavor. This setting may see diminished levels of trust, commitment, and satisfaction among team members, along with reduced social support and emotional well-being. To counter these challenges, there is a heightened need for effective communication and collaboration techniques aimed at fostering team cohesion. Facing these challenges head-on, a leader must ask: How can they foster team cohesion in a setting where team members may never meet in person or know each other only superficially due to limited interactions? The answer lies in understanding and implementing strategies that can replicate in a virtual environment, to some extent, the cohesion-building aspects of physical teams.

Local team:
- Natural opportunities for team bonding.
- Easier to build a shared culture and values.
- Easier to build team cohesion based on shared identity, values, and norms.
- More trust, commitment, and satisfaction among team members.
- More social support and emotional well-being for team members.

Remote team:
- Requires deliberate effort to build team cohesion.
- Risk of isolation or lack of shared culture.
- Harder to build team cohesion based on shared identity, values, and norms.
- Less trust, commitment, and satisfaction among team members.
- Less social support and emotional well-being for team members.
- More need for communication and collaboration to foster team cohesion.

A study[21] by Jacqueline Mueller, Robbie Matz, Zack J. Damon, Michael L. Naraine, and James Skinner explores the impact of physical proximity on team cohesion. It underscores the importance of physical interactions and shared experiences in building a cohesive team, highlighting the challenges and potential solutions for fostering team cohesion in remote or distributed teams.

Later in this book, I will unfold a series of practices designed to foster team cohesion via social good initiatives and community-building efforts. These insights will illuminate how, despite the inherent challenges and the need for extra effort, a great leader can effectively cultivate a sense of unity and collaboration within a remote or gig-based ecosystem.

Work-life balance

The concept of work-life balance in team management reveals stark contrasts when comparing local teams to remote or gig-freelancer teams.

Local teams often enjoy a clearer demarcation between work and personal life. The physical separation of office and home naturally helps in maintaining this boundary. It is generally easier for managers and peers in such settings to respect reasonable working hours, allowing team members to establish and adhere to clear routines. Moreover, local teams typically have more direct access to organizational resources and policies designed to support work-life balance.

On the other hand, remote teams, including those comprised of gig-freelancers, face the ongoing challenge of blurred lines between their professional and personal lives. The flexibility inherent in remote work, while advantageous in many ways, can paradoxically lead to overwork. Remote team members often find it more challenging to establish and maintain clear boundaries and routines. There is also a noted disparity in the respect and understanding of work-life balance among leaders, managers, and peers in remote settings, coupled with less access to organizational resources that support this balance. In such environments, the need for self-management and the negotiation of work-life balance become more pronounced.

A local team manager might strictly adhere to regular work hours and respect personal time, avoiding expectations of overtime or weekend work. In contrast, a leader managing a remote team needs to respect the diverse work preferences and personal circumstances of their team members, ensuring they are not expected to be available indiscriminately.

Local team:
- Clearer boundary between work and personal life.
- Easier to ensure reasonable work hours.
- Easier to separate work and personal life and maintain clear boundaries and routines.
- More respect and understanding for work-life balance among leaders, managers, and peers.
- More access to organizational resources and policies that support work-life balance.

Remote team:
- Risk of blurring boundaries between work and personal life.
- Flexibility may lead to overwork.
- Harder to separate work and personal life and maintain clear boundaries and routines.
- Less respect and understanding for work-life balance among leaders, managers, and peers.
- Less access to organizational resources and policies that support work-life balance.
- More need for self-management and negotiation of work-life balance.

A study[22] by Melika Shirmohammadi, Wee Chan Au, and Mina Beigi delves into the impact of remote work on work-life balance during the COVID-19 pandemic. It provides insights and suggestions for Human Resource Development practitioners on how to enhance work-life balance in remote settings, emphasizing the importance of setting clear boundaries between work and personal life.

Many managers, previously successful in managing their teams, have faced significant challenges in maintaining a work-life balance when transitioning to fully remote operations. The lack of a fundamental care component in their leadership approach led to increased friction between managers and workers. These managers struggled to adapt to the new remote working environment, often finding themselves at a loss on how to effectively manage the situation.

The quality of caring in a leader becomes particularly crucial and influential in remote and gig-freelancing scenarios. A caring leader is adept at sending clear signals and providing the necessary resources to ensure that their remote team maintains a healthy work-life balance. While it is understood that there may be occasions where overtime or working under pressure is required, the true skill of a caring leader lies in the ability to inspire team members to willingly and enthusiastically contribute extra effort when necessary. This is not about imposing demands but rather about fostering a team environment where people are motivated to go above and beyond, not out of obligation but out of a sense of commitment and trust in their leader.

In the upcoming sections of this discussion, we will delve deeper into this topic, exploring it through various stories and practical suggestions. These narratives and insights will be especially valuable for leaders who find themselves steering unknown teams. The aim is to equip these leaders with strategies and approaches that not only enhance the performance of their teams but also nurture a culture where team members feel genuinely supported and valued. This balance is key to achieving not only high productivity but also fostering a sense of well-being and satisfaction among team members, crucial elements in the success of any remote or gig-based workforce.

Trust building

Trust building is vital in leadership as it shapes organizational culture, enriches communication, and boosts employee engagement. When leaders are trustworthy, it fosters an environment of honesty and integrity, encouraging ethical behavior and a sense of security among employees. This trust also leads to open and transparent communication, enabling employees to share ideas and feedback freely. In such an atmosphere, employee satisfaction increases as team members feel valued and heard, leading to higher engagement and productivity. Additionally, trust is crucial for effective collaboration, driving innovation, and problem-solving by allowing diverse ideas to merge harmoniously. It also plays a key role in managing change, as employees are more likely to embrace new directions and strategies from leaders they trust. Ultimately, trust contributes significantly to the overall success and sustainability of an organization, making it an indispensable aspect of effective leadership.

Building trust in a local team often benefits from the advantage of face-to-face interactions. Physical proximity allows for more natural opportunities to demonstrate integrity and transparency. Trust in this environment is frequently based on interpersonal interactions, shared experiences, and a mutual understanding that is easier to establish and maintain. This foundation tends to foster more credibility, reliability, and intimacy among team members, leading to increased cooperation and collaboration.

In contrast, the landscape of trust building in remote teams presents a more complex picture. The absence of physical interaction and shared daily experiences makes it harder to build trust based on interpersonal dynamics and shared understanding. This lack of direct contact often results in reduced credibility, reliability, and intimacy among team members, posing a challenge to cooperation and collaboration. Consequently, there is a greater need for deliberate communication and feedback to establish and maintain trust.

Local team:
- Easier to build trust through face-to-face interactions.
- Natural opportunities to demonstrate integrity and transparency.
- Easier to build trust based on interpersonal interactions, shared experiences, and mutual understanding.

- More credibility, reliability, and intimacy among team members.
- More cooperation and collaboration based on trust.

Remote team:
- Harder to build trust based on interpersonal interactions, shared experiences, and mutual understanding.
- Less credibility, reliability, and intimacy among team members.
- Less cooperation and collaboration based on trust.
- More need for communication and feedback to build trust.

How important is real leadership in trust building? And how important is trust when it comes to extraordinary results? Many publications exist about those concepts.

There is an interesting blog post[23] on Knolskape's website that outlines six leadership approaches that are crucial for building trust in remote teams. The first of these approaches is exercising vulnerability, which fosters trust and ensures that the organization runs smoothly, even in a distributed work setting. The second one shows us a trustworthy leader by keeping actions and statements in sync. The third one, which exposes the caring of the leader, is to take ownership when things go wrong and help resolve those difficulties. For those who are not natural-born leaders, the challenge of genuinely caring about a difficult problem, particularly when leading a remote team, can be daunting. It is temptingly easy to adopt a laissez-faire attitude, shrugging off the issue with a casual "let it go." This tendency is even more pronounced when the team member facing the problem is a distant gig-freelancer. In such cases, many managers might conveniently choose to "delegate" the hardship, passing the problem to someone far removed from their immediate sphere. A fundamental approach I firmly believe in and is very important to execute is the fourth approach, which discusses developing emotional intelligence. The fifth approach emphasizes rapid adaptation to change, advocating for proactive leadership in evolving work dynamics, especially in managing remote teams, and stresses on organization-wide engagement in fostering a culture of curiosity, innovation, and readiness for change to ensure long-term success. The sixth and final one is all about celebrating the achievements and initiatives, no matter how tiny they might be.

Collaboration

Collaboration is a cornerstone of effective team dynamics, but it manifests differently in local and remote team settings. This section aims to dissect and understand these differences at a high level, offering insights into the distinct challenges and opportunities that arise when fostering teamwork in varied environments.

In local teams, the advantage of natural, face-to-face interactions creates an ecosystem where idea sharing and collaboration occur more organically. Being co-located, these teams can quickly iterate, prototype, and collaborate on projects with relative ease. This proximity not only facilitates the sharing of ideas and problem-solving but also fosters more creativity and innovation, drawing from the diverse perspectives within the team. Moreover, co-located teams often experience greater alignment and coordination, with the shared physical space enhancing the synchronicity of team efforts.

Conversely, remote teams, including those with gig-freelancers, face more significant hurdles in these areas. Collaboration on projects, idea sharing, and problem-solving can be more challenging due to the lack of physical proximity. These teams often witness less creativity and innovation from diverse perspectives and experience reduced alignment and coordination among members. The reliance on technology and tools becomes more pronounced in these settings, requiring a different approach to foster effective collaboration.

A local team manager might encourage in-house team members to engage in brainstorming sessions, experimentation, and mutual learning, capitalizing on the immediacy of physical interaction. On the other hand, a remote team leader must create a collaborative culture using digital tools such as Microsoft Teams, OneDrive, Office, Google Docs, Slack, and Zoom. These tools become the conduits through which remote teams connect, share ideas, and work together.

Local team:
- Natural interactions can lead to organic idea-sharing.
- Co-located teams can quickly iterate and prototype.
- Easier to collaborate on projects, share ideas, and solve problems.
- More creativity and innovation from diverse perspectives.
- More alignment and coordination among team members.

Remote team:
- Harder to collaborate on projects, share ideas, and solve problems.
- Less creativity and innovation from diverse perspectives.
- Less alignment and coordination among team members.
- More dependence on technology and tools.

A great article named "Uncovering the complexities of remote leadership and the usage of digital tools during the COVID-19 pandemic: A qualitative diary study" by Eva-Helen Krehl and Marion Büttagen[24] identifies four categories of leadership practices crucial for remote teams:

- Solving problems collaboratively and monitoring team progress.
- Creating space for socializing and teambuilding
- Make the team feel supported and encourage

feedback.

- Communicating to build a virtual culture of trust.

Understanding and implementing these practices is key to overcoming the inherent challenges of remote collaboration. While technology provides the platform, it is the leader's approach and skill in using these tools that determine the effectiveness of collaboration in remote settings.

Adaptability

Adaptability in team leadership takes on distinctive shades when comparing local teams with remote or gig-freelancer teams.

Local teams may exhibit a slower pace in adapting to changes or new technologies due to established routines and physical constraints. However, they often find it easier to adapt to changing situations, demands, and expectations, and managing resistance to change can be more straightforward. These teams typically demonstrate more resilience and agility, benefiting from the direct feedback and experimentation possible in a co-located environment. In-person training and support for change management further aid in enhancing their adaptability. Communication is more fluid and direct, and this helps local teams adapt to changes in direction faster, in general, than remote teams.

In contrast, remote teams might inherently be more adaptable to change and new technologies, thanks in part to their virtual nature and necessity for constant evolution. However, addressing resistance or challenges in adaptability can be more complex due to the lack of physical presence and direct interaction. These teams may experience less resilience and agility, with fewer opportunities for learning and innovations based on immediate feedback and experimentation. Trust and empowerment become crucial factors in fostering adaptability in these environments, alongside opportunities for virtual training and support.

A local team manager may focus on encouraging their in-house team members to embrace change, learn from failure, and experiment with new approaches. Similarly, a leader of a remote team would need to instill these same values, albeit through different methodologies and communication strategies.

Local team:
- May be slower to adapt to changes or new technologies.
- Easier to adapt to changing situations, demands, and expectations. Easier to manage resistance to change.
- More resilience and agility among team members.
- More learning and innovation from feedback and experimentation.
- In-person training and support for change management.

Remote team:
- May be more adaptable to change and new technologies.
- Possible resistance or adaptability challenges may be harder to address.
- Less resilience and agility among team members.
- Less learning and innovation from feedback and experimentation.
- More need for trust and empowerment to foster adaptability.

I have observed a stark contrast in how managers and true leaders handle their teams. Managers often find themselves drained trying to get their local teams to embrace change and adaptability. It is an exhausting endeavor. On the other hand, I have seen caring leaders effortlessly guide their remote, unknown teams through change and adaptability with minimal exertion. The difference? It boils down to the innate element of caring leadership. I am skeptical about the effectiveness of expensive leadership courses or devouring countless leadership books in instilling this quality. They might offer some insight, but the transformation they promise often falls short, especially in the mid-term.

A study[25] published on the Velocity Global website referring to a Harvard Business School survey where 71% of 1,500 executives from more than 90 countries said adaptability was the most important leadership quality. The study elaborates on the importance of adaptability in changing work environments, especially in remote and global teams. It discusses how adaptability can help navigate staff changes, new remote work policies, and other changes, thereby fostering a culture of resilience and continuous learning.

The critical point here is the necessity for organizations to meticulously assess and select leaders, particularly for guiding unknown teams. This selection should prioritize the inherent qualities of a caring leader over simply choosing a good or experienced manager and attempting to train them for the role. Leadership, especially in remote and dynamic environments, requires more than just experience: it demands an intrinsic ability to connect, empathize, and inspire qualities that are not easily taught but are essential in guiding teams effectively.

"Leadership is the capacity to translate vision into reality."
Warren Bennis

Unlocking Success in Leading the Unknown Teams

Managing or leading teams comes in several distinct flavors. The first type is a fully local team, where all members are housed in the same facility, building, or location. This proximity allows for easy face-to-face interactions, casual coffee conversations, and social activities like local gatherings or pizza parties. Then there is the hybrid team. In this model, some team members are on-site while others work remotely. The remote team members might be in the same geographical area as the on-site ones or in entirely different locations. This setup blends local and remote dynamics, requiring a balance in communication and engagement strategies. The third type is a fully remote team. Here, every team member works remotely, either in the same region as the leader or manager or spread across the country or even the globe. This scenario demands a high level of digital communication proficiency and a strong online presence from the leader to maintain cohesion and morale.

Often overlooked in many leadership books and training courses is the fourth type: teams comprising entirely of freelancers-gig workers who operate remotely. This scenario can also extend to an organization with a workforce that is largely unknown to the leadership in a traditional sense. These teams present unique challenges in building trust, establishing communication norms, and creating a sense of team identity, given the lack of physical interaction and the often-transient nature of gig work. The leadership approach here needs to be even more adaptive, empathetic, and innovative to manage and inspire such a diverse and dispersed group effectively.

The following sections are crafted to offer an expansive reflection on the wealth of knowledge I have gathered and to share a curated selection of practices and methodologies that have stood the test of time. These insights are drawn from my substantial tenure of more than half a decade in organizing exceptionally successful, geographically dispersed freelancing teams, operating in the dynamic and ever-evolving gig economy. This narrative spans the prelude and the subsequent transformation of the corporate landscape brought on by the COVID-19 pandemic. It is a story of resilience, adaptation, and triumph in the face of a paradigm shift toward remote collaboration and leadership.

Through this discourse, I aim to dissect the elements that have been instrumental in navigating the complexities and nuances of virtual team management, fostering cohesion, and driving productivity in a world where traditional office boundaries have been redefined.

"Leadership is not about being in charge. It is about taking care of those in your charge."
Simon Sinek

Core Leadership Qualities and Approaches

Leading unknown teams in the contemporary landscape of remote and gig-freelancer workforces demands a shift from traditional leadership styles to a more purpose-centric and empathetic approach. This new paradigm of leadership is not just about managing tasks but about nurturing a shared vision that transcends physical distances and cultural differences. It involves creating a narrative that binds the team together, rooted in the history and legacy of the organization. In this context, leadership is less about exerting authority and more about fostering an environment of authenticity and mutual respect. It is a delicate balance of being humble yet inspiring, where leaders are not just commanders but facilitators who enable each team member to connect, contribute, and grow. This approach redefines leadership as a journey of collective success, where every individual feels valued and purposefully engaged.

1. Purpose as a key driver

The intersection of purpose and care in leadership is a profound concept, and several influential books have delved into this topic, offering insights and guidance to leaders seeking to foster a caring environment driven by a clear sense of purpose. One such book is *The Art of Caring Leadership* by Heather R. Younger, which explores how leaders can create a culture of engagement and loyalty through empathy and understanding. The book emphasizes the importance of leaders who genuinely care for their teams, which in turn can inspire employees to care not just for their work but for the collective vision and mission of the organization. Another book that touches on the fabric of leadership and culture is *Tribal Leadership* by Dave Logan, John King, and Halee Fischer-Wright. This book provides a blueprint for building work cultures that yield results. It underlines the importance of a strong corporate culture, which, when correctly nurtured, naturally results in excellent customer service and a robust brand. This aligns with the belief that if the culture, which is a manifestation of the organization's purpose and care, is right, other aspects like customer service will naturally follow. The principles outlined in this book were notably applied by Tony Hsieh at Zappos, prioritizing culture as a key to success.

Simon Sinek's *Start With Why* further emphasizes the role of purpose in leadership. Sinek, in his book, argues that understanding the "why" behind actions is crucial for inspiring true leadership. He contends that people and organizations that start with "why" tend to be more innovative, influential, and profitable. They command greater loyalty from customers and employees alike because their purpose is clear, and they care about it more than just the end result.

Collectively, these books underscore that caring leadership, grounded in a well-articulated and embraced purpose, is critical for any organization's longevity and success. They provide a framework and practical examples demonstrating how purpose-driven care in leadership can not only drive success but also create a sustainable, positive impact on employees and the larger community.

When Satya Nadella stepped into the role of CEO at Microsoft in 2014, he brought with him a vision that was as transformative as it was purposeful. His leadership philosophy was encapsulated in the belief that technology should empower everyone on the planet to achieve more. But more than a mere corporate tagline, this vision became the heartbeat of Microsoft under his tenure. Nadella's approach was grounded in the idea that innovation, not tradition, drives the tech industry. He famously said: "Our industry does not respect tradition. It only respects innovation." This mindset led to a strategic shift at Microsoft, moving away from a sole focus on Windows to embracing cloud computing and AI technologies, and the purpose he seeded in the hearts of the employees, no matter where and who, led to outstanding outcomes.

A key aspect of Nadella's leadership was learning from failures. He acknowledged: "When I think about my career, my successes are built on learning from failures." This philosophy created a culture where experimentation and learning were valued over sticking to the tried and true. It was about staying relevant and forward-thinking, a necessity in the ever-evolving tech landscape. One remarkable example of Nadella's purpose-driven leadership was the development of the Seeing AI app. This tool was designed to assist visually impaired individuals, reflecting Nadella's commitment to using technology for social good. It was a powerful illustration of how a clear, purpose-driven vision can lead to innovative and impactful products. Nadella's approach was also about building a culture based on empathy and understanding. He believed in the power of listening, stating: "Listening was the most important thing I accomplished each day because it would build the foundation of leadership for years to come." His leadership style was not about command and control but about understanding the needs of both customers and employees and responding to them with vision, purpose, and innovation.

Under Nadella, Microsoft did not just grow in financial terms; it also underwent a cultural transformation. This change was not just about achieving business success but about making a positive impact on the world, thus truly embodying the principle of purpose in leadership. Nadella managed to expose his purpose in every act and every speech at every opportunity, and hence, not only Microsoft employees spread across the planet followed his purpose but also partners, customers, and shareholders.

Another great example of leading with purpose is Paul Polman and his leadership at Unilever. Paul Polman, during his tenure as CEO of Unilever, revolutionized the way corporations can embrace sustainability while remaining profitable. His principle of purpose was clear: businesses should focus on improving the lives of the world's citizens and creating sustainable solutions. Polman believed that by aligning with consumer and societal needs, a company could achieve better shareholder returns, stating: "What we firmly believe in is that if we focus our company on improving the lives of the world's citizens and come up with genuinely sustainable solutions, we are more in synch with consumers and society and ultimately this will result in good shareholder returns." He implemented this vision through the Unilever Sustainable Living Plan, which aimed to decouple the company's growth from its environmental footprint. This initiative was groundbreaking, showcasing Polman's belief in leadership as a tool for unleashing other people's energy and investing in others. He said: "The moment you discover in life that it is not about yourself, that it is about investing in others, I think you are entering a steadier state to be a great leader."

Polman's strategy was not without challenges. The corporate world often leans towards short-term gains, but he advocated for long-term, sustainable strategies. He emphasized the importance of continuous learning and unlearning old practices, noting: "This world is changing enormously. In any position in a company, you need to work very hard on learning new skills every day, but you also need to unlearn some of the old skills from the past." Under Polman, Unilever made bold commitments like sourcing 100% of its agricultural raw materials sustainably. This not only bolstered Unilever's brand reputation but also positively influenced the broader market and supply chain towards sustainability.

Polman's leadership at Unilever serves as a beacon for how a purpose-driven approach can create a balance between profit and social conscience, proving that businesses can be a force for good in the world.

Beginning with the "why" has been a cornerstone of my approach from the very first day I interact with any gig-freelancer. Emphasizing this fundamental aspect is crucial. When an individual grasps the "why" behind their work and hears it directly from their leader right at the outset, the effect is markedly noticeable. This initial understanding sets the tone for their engagement and commitment, making a tangible difference in how they perceive and approach their tasks.

Throughout my tenure, I have had the privilege of guiding thousands of freelancers within IT operations, personally initiating their journey from the very first day. The onboarding experience, where I extend a warm welcome into our vast corporate family, begins with an essential narrative: the "why" of our organization's existence, its purposeful mission. This "why" is, in my view, the magnetic force that unites disparate individuals from the onset. It is the foundation that helps build a common identity. Like a flag, it unites many people from different backgrounds into a focused group of professionals.

2. History as a glue

The history of an organization, be it a corporate entity, a business venture, a collective of people, or a tribal alliance, serves as a potent adhesive, bonding diverse individuals to a shared quest. It is a rich narrative crafted from tales of past challenges, triumphs over adversity, and the heralding of legendary figures whose contributions have become the lore of the workplace. These stories, key milestones, and the arc of growth and achievement are meticulously chronicled and presented. This storytelling ritual begins on day one of induction, where newcomers, be they remote contributors, gig workers, or freelancers, are immersed in the organization's legacy. Each retelling at successive junctures reinforces this narrative. Such practices foster a profound sense of belonging, as every fresh face is seamlessly engrafted into the ongoing epic, inspired by the prospect of being an integral part of this grand story that will be recounted for generations to follow.

Take the Walt Disney Company; its history is like a magical adventure. It all started with Walt Disney himself, a man with big dreams and a whole lot of creativity. Back in the 1920s, he set up a little studio, and even though it was not easy at first, he never gave up on making people happy through his stories and cartoons. Disney's big break came with Mickey Mouse and the movie "Steamboat Willie," which was a huge success. Then came "Snow White and the Seven Dwarfs," the first-ever full-length animated movie, and it was amazing. People loved it, and it opened the door for all the Disney movies we know and love today. But Walt Disney did not stop there. He had an even bigger dream: Disneyland. In 1955, he turned that dream into reality and created a place where families could have fun and experience the magic of Disney in real life. Disneyland was not just a theme park; it was a place where Walt's dream of making people happy came to life.

As time went on, Disney grew into this huge company that makes movies and TV shows and has theme parks all over the world. They kept coming up with new ideas and stories, like when they joined forces with Pixar, Marvel, and Lucasfilm to reach an even wider audience. For people who work at Disney, the company's story is really inspiring. It teaches them to keep going, even when things get tough, and to always think of new and fun ways to tell stories. It is not just about being part of a big company; it is about being part of a story that has brought joy to so many people.

Disney's story is a reminder that when you follow your dreams and put your heart into them, amazing things can happen. It is all about making people happy and creating memories that last forever. For everyone who works at Disney, they are not just doing a job; they are part of a magical journey that keeps bringing smiles to people's faces, generation after generation. Imagine on your first day, during your onboarding, Walt Disney Company's CEO joins the welcome session for 10 minutes and inspiringly tells you about the Disney story. This is a goose-bumping experience, making someone want to conquer the universe and become part of this story.

Relaying the history of our organization during remote onboarding sessions has always filled me with immense pride. It is a practice that not only instills a sense of belonging but also reignites my own connection with our collective journey, triumphs, and trials alike. My heart opens fully as I share these memories, especially with the diverse remote workers who join our ranks. I vividly recount stories of solidarity in the face of adversity, milestones that marked our growth, and the individual achievements that embody our principles, like the remote worker who built homes in Central Africa for orphan children or when the organization achieved a 40% female workforce in the tech domain, a notable feat.

These stories, told from the start and whenever possible, connect deeply with everyone. They inspire all workers, even those far away, to add their own experiences to our shared story. The consistent, positive feedback only underscores the profound impact of these stories. They are not just tales; they are affirmations of our shared humanity and proof of the caring leadership that values every step of our collective journey.

As a side note, it is often observed that many managers, even in a local setup, might forget the crucial welcoming sessions, citing a high volume of commitments and limited time availability.

3. Creating authentic connections in the workplace

In any organization, a true leader stands out distinctly from a typical manager. It is not just about strategies or goals; it is about the ability to forge genuine, spontaneous connections with people across all levels of the organization. This approach, especially crucial in today's remote and freelance work environments, makes a profound difference in creating a thriving, connected, and motivated workplace. True leadership is characterized by its focus on authentic, ad-hoc interactions. Unlike traditional managers who might limit their interactions to a select few within predefined contexts, a true leader reaches out indiscriminately, connecting with individuals regardless of their role, rank, or background. There is something special about these spontaneous interactions, whether it is a message, a chat, or a call, that can evolve into meaningful relationships.

Imagine a leader who doesn't just talk business but starts by asking, "How are you really doing?" This simple question can lead to deeper understanding and collaboration, transcending traditional work relationships. For example, consider a CEO who personally calls new employees within their first week, not to discuss work but to genuinely welcome them and understand their aspirations. Or a leader who regularly joins different team chats or virtual coffee breaks, not with an agenda, but simply to listen and be present. Another inspiring example is a leader in a multinational corporation who sets up informal walk-and-talk virtual meetings. These meetings are not about work; they are about connecting on a personal level, sharing life stories, challenges, and experiences, breaking down hierarchical barriers, and fostering a sense of belonging and mutual respect. The walk-and-talk practice, which traditionally involves conducting meetings while walking to foster open dialogue and creativity, can be adapted for remote work environments in various ways. In a virtual setting, this can include having meetings where participants walk in their own spaces while conversing over the phone or recording voice memos for asynchronous discussions. Additionally, encouraging movement breaks during long virtual meetings or initiating team challenges related to walking can simulate the benefits of the walk-and-talk approach, enhancing energy, creativity, and a sense of community within remote teams.

The difference between a caring leader and a typical manager becomes evident when these genuine interactions are contrasted with ones that feel forced or strategic. We have all experienced interactions where someone inquires about our well-being only to swiftly pivot to a work-related favor. While the gesture is appreciated, the underlying intention often feels transparent, leaving the interaction feeling somewhat disingenuous. A true leader, however, does not always talk about work in scheduled interactions. Instead, they seek to understand how people in their organization are genuinely doing, creating deeper, more intimate connections. When a leader reaches out authentically, it resonates far beyond that single conversation. People feel valued and seen, not just as employees or workers, but as individuals. They talk about these interactions with peers, friends, and family, enhancing the organization's culture. This approach builds trust, fosters loyalty, and nurtures a supportive environment where everyone feels part of a larger community.

The essence of genuine leadership lies in creating these authentic connections every day. It is about transcending the traditional confines of a managerial role and embracing the role of a leader who cares, listens, and connects. In an age where work dynamics are rapidly evolving, this approach to leadership can be a beacon, guiding organizations toward a more connected, empathetic, and successful future.

The co-founder of Southwest Airlines, Herb Kelleher, was famous for his unconventional leadership style. He knew many of his employees by name and would frequently be seen engaging with them in a down-to-earth, personal manner. His genuine care for the workforce was a key factor in building Southwest's strong corporate culture.

Although not a corporate example, the Antarctic explorer Ernest Shackleton's leadership during the ill-fated Imperial Trans-Antarctic Expedition between 1914 and 1917 is legendary. When his ship, Endurance, was trapped and later crushed by ice, Shackleton's priority was his crew's welfare. He worked tirelessly to keep morale high, often engaging with each crew member, understanding their state of mind, and ensuring their well-being, which was crucial for their incredible survival.

One of the U.S. presidents, Abraham Lincoln, was known for his accessibility and connection with the citizens during the Civil War. He often held open-door sessions at the White House, where he would listen to the concerns and stories of ordinary citizens. This approach helped him stay connected with the realities of the nation he was leading.

As the CEO who saved Xerox from bankruptcy, Anne Mulcahy is often praised for her leadership style, which included genuine, direct communication with employees at all levels. She reportedly visited numerous Xerox offices and facilities, engaging in frank conversations with employees, understanding their concerns, and involving them in the company's turnaround strategy. In her conversations, despite Xerox's financial situation, she prioritized the people's well-being over the company's situation, which really made a difference. As people discovered her genuine approach, they helped her and the company, leading it towards success.

Personalized relationships in such organizations do matter, and they matter more in remote work setups. I personally have been connecting with coworkers in my organization this way, and the results have been more than satisfactory, creating deep bonds between me and the people with whom I connected. A bond that would go beyond the work relationship and become a true friendship.

4. Humbleness

Being humble is a trait often lauded by leaders, yet it remains an elusive quality, shrouded in mystery and debate. The essence of humility lies in a leader's ability to place others' needs and recognition above their own, to admit mistakes, and to be open to feedback and learning. This characteristic becomes particularly vital in the context of remote organizations or those comprising gig workers and freelancers, where the traditional paradigms of leadership are constantly challenged.

The digital landscape of remote work demands a leader who can navigate through the complexities of virtual communication with empathy and understanding. In such settings, a humble leader stands out by actively listening to the individuals in the team no matter their role or location, acknowledging the diverse challenges faced by remote workers, and valuing each contribution regardless of its scale or the conventional hierarchy. This approach fosters an environment of mutual respect and collective growth, which is essential for the fluid and dynamic nature of gig and freelance work. However, the root of this discussion delves into the nature versus nurture debate: Are leaders born with humility, or can it be cultivated over time through life experiences? While it is undeniable that life's journey can profoundly impact a person's character, shaping them to be more understanding and empathetic, the argument here is that the seed of humility must already exist within an individual's inherent makeup.

My perspective and experience suggest that humility, much like other intrinsic traits, is woven into the very DNA of a person. It implies that a truly humble leader doesn't just adopt this characteristic over time; rather, they are naturally inclined towards selflessness and empathy from the outset. Their life experiences and challenges may refine this trait, making it more apparent and effective in their leadership style, but the fundamental capacity for humility is innate.

This intrinsic humility becomes a cornerstone for successful leadership in remote or gig-freelancing setups. It enables leaders to bridge the gap created by physical distances, building a culture of trust and open communication. These leaders, with their inherent humility, instinctively understand the nuances of leading a dispersed team, recognizing the individual struggles and aspirations of their members, and guiding them with a gentle, unassuming hand.

While life experiences can undoubtedly enhance and bring forth a leader's humility, the contention that this trait is ingrained in one's very nature holds significant weight. Such inborn humility is especially pivotal in the unique and evolving landscapes of remote organizations and freelance collectives, where traditional leadership styles falter, and a deeper, more intrinsic understanding of empathy and selflessness becomes the key to effective and caring leadership.

The value of a humble leader in the corporate world cannot be overstated. A leader who openly admits mistakes and learns from them is not just admirable but essential. After all, we are all human beings, each with different roles, and the role of a leader is, as the title suggests, to lead.

In my corporate career, I have observed various leadership styles. I have seen numerous managers who, unfortunately, exhibited arrogance and ego, letting these traits overshadow their potential. However, I have also had the opportunity to work with leaders who, despite their vast knowledge and success, exuded humility. Their demeanor, actions, and words garnered deep respect due to their humble nature. These humble leaders celebrated not just successes but also the learnings that emerged from mistakes. This approach fostered a culture of confidence and understanding, emphasizing that mistakes and failures are acceptable, provided we learn and grow from them.

Leading a remote or gig freelancer organization presents unique challenges in terms of humility compared to leading a full-time employee or local team. For remote and gig leaders, the key difficulty lies in building trust and rapport without the benefit of physical presence. Humility becomes crucial in these settings as it helps in acknowledging the diverse challenges faced by remote workers and validating their contributions, regardless of their contractual status or location.

Conversely, leaders of local teams often have the advantage of face-to-face interactions, which can make it easier to establish authority and rapport. However, this proximity can sometimes lead to a false sense of control or superiority, challenging the leader's ability to remain humble.

For remote and gig leaders, demonstrating humility often requires more deliberate effort. They need to be intentional in their communications, ensuring that their respect and appreciation for their team's efforts are clearly conveyed despite the lack of physical interaction. This might involve regularly scheduled virtual meetings, personalized feedback, and public acknowledgment of team members' contributions.

In contrast, leaders of local teams can more readily demonstrate humility through everyday interactions, like being physically present in difficult situations or participating in team activities. Their challenge is to maintain humility in an environment where traditional hierarchical structures are more visible and can reinforce a sense of superiority.

The core principles of humble leadership, such as prioritizing others, embracing a learning mindset, and recognizing personal limitations, remain consistent. However, the ways in which these principles are put into practice and the unique challenges encountered can differ significantly in the contexts of remote/gig and local/full-time leadership.

Throughout my career, I have had the opportunity to work with a diverse range of individuals in management positions, ranging from those who simply held the title of manager to those who truly embodied the qualities of exceptional leadership. The most impactful among these were the humble leaders, those who inspired confidence to follow them anywhere. These leaders have been instrumental in my professional growth, imparting more wisdom and insight than their less humble counterparts.

My personal journey has taught me the value of humility in leadership. On several occasions, I have chosen to move away from managers who exhibited arrogant behavior. Such individuals often struggled with accepting feedback, acknowledging different viewpoints, and practicing equitable recognition of team efforts. Their tendency to take sole credit for team successes and place blame on team members for failures created a challenging work environment. This experience underscored for me the importance of leadership qualities like humility, openness to feedback, and the ability to recognize and celebrate the contributions of the entire team.

5. Inspiring everyone in the organization

As a leader of a global team of remote and gig workers, witnessing the evolution of remote work and the gig economy over the years, I have consistently drawn inspiration and guidance from the wisdom of history's most influential figures. Their insights, encapsulating the depths of human experience and wisdom, have not only molded me into a better professional but also a more insightful and compassionate person.

Take, for instance, Winston Churchill's stirring words, "Success is not final, failure is not fatal: It is the courage to continue that counts." This quote has served as a guiding light in my leadership journey, reminding me that the path to success is non-linear and that perseverance is key. Churchill, a man who steered a nation through its darkest hour, knew the weight of these words. In the face of the inevitable setbacks and challenges of managing a remote workforce, where physical distance can often translate into emotional disconnect, Churchill's wisdom has been a source of inspiration, guiding me to foster resilience and steadfastness, not only for myself but also for my teams.

Similarly, Nelson Mandela's powerful assertion: "It always seems impossible until it is done.", has been a mantra for me during moments of doubt and uncertainty. Mandela, the epitome of determination and resilience, faced seemingly insurmountable challenges with grace and fortitude. His journey inspires to approach each project, each challenge, with a mindset that no mountain is too high to climb. In the complex structure of global remote work, where each day brings new challenges, Mandela's words remind me and my team to embrace the impossible as simply the yet-to-be-achieved.

The wisdom of Marie Curie: "Be less curious about people and more curious about ideas.", has also been integral in shaping my approach to leadership. Curie, a trailblazer in science, understood the value of nurturing ideas and innovation. In the context of remote work, where collaboration is key, this perspective has helped me focus on harnessing the collective intellectual power of my team, encouraging a culture where ideas are valued over hierarchy, thus fostering a more inclusive and dynamic work environment.

Steve Jobs, a visionary who redefined the technological landscape, once said: "The people who are crazy enough to think they can change the world are the ones who do." This quote is prominently displayed as my computer wallpaper, serving as a daily reminder of the power of vision and innovation. In leading a global team, this quote constantly pushes me to think outside the box, to inspire my team to be trailblazers, and to remember that groundbreaking work often begins with a single, seemingly crazy idea.

Lastly, Albert Einstein's advice: "Try not to become a man of success, but rather try to become a man of value." resonates deeply with me. Einstein, whose contributions to physics changed our understanding of the universe, reminds me that true leadership is about creating value for the team, the organization, and the broader community. In the fast-paced, result-oriented world of remote work, this quote keeps me grounded, ensuring that my leadership style is not just about achieving targets but also about nurturing a work culture that values ethical practices, personal growth, and social responsibility.

Each of these quotes, adorning my walls, my digital spaces, and most importantly, etched in my mind, have been a source of strength and inspiration. They have lifted me from moments of despair, rekindled my motivation when exhaustion seemed overwhelming, and reminded me that my role as a leader is part of a larger purpose. By embodying the wisdom of these great minds, I strive to become a better version of myself every day, guiding my team toward a future where our collective efforts transcend geographical boundaries to make a meaningful impact.

The question of how, as a leader, I could ignite change within an organization comprising over a thousand individuals scattered across the globe and multiple time zones, evolved into a formidable challenge. I did not mirror the grandeur of those historical figures whose words echo through time, nor did I view myself as particularly inspirational or charismatic. Yet, amidst this self-reflection, I harbored a strategy.

I began reflecting on the individuals who had inspired me, pondering over what made them so inspirational. I meticulously examined the lives of those who influenced me the most, focusing on their approach to challenging circumstances, their methods of handling these situations, and, critically, their communication style with others. I delved into the nature of the messages they conveyed, the timing of their delivery, and the reasons behind their communication choices.

These five individuals, Winston Churchill, Nelson Mandela, Marie Curie, Steve Jobs, and Albert Einstein, despite their diverse backgrounds and fields, share several commonalities in their lives:

Overcoming adversity

Each of the previously mentioned characters faced significant challenges and adversities. Churchill led Britain through World War II, Mandela fought against apartheid and was imprisoned, Curie dealt with the challenges of being a female scientist in the early 20th century, Jobs was ousted from Apple before returning to transform it, and Einstein fled Nazi Germany due to his Jewish heritage.

Innovative thinking
They were all innovative thinkers. Churchill's leadership during wartime, Mandela's approach to peace and reconciliation, Curie's pioneering research in radioactivity, Jobs' innovative spirit, and Einstein's groundbreaking theories in physics all required thinking beyond conventional norms.

Lasting impact
Each left a lasting impact on the world. Their contributions – whether in politics, science, technology, or human rights, have had a profound and enduring effect on societies and industries globally.

Global recognition and respect
They all received global recognition and respect for their work. This includes Nobel Prizes and Time's Person of the Year.

Inspiring leadership
All were leaders in their respective fields, inspiring others through their actions and words. Their leadership was not just positional but also moral and intellectual, influencing people's thoughts and actions worldwide.

Additionally, there's a common theme in the quotes I mentioned earlier. Here's my interpretation:

Resilience in the face of adversity
Each quote emphasizes the importance of perseverance and resilience. They reflect an understanding that success often comes after overcoming challenges and failures.

Inspiration and aspiration
The quotes are all motivational, encouraging individuals to aspire for greater things, whether it is making a significant change in the

world, pursuing innovative ideas, or aiming for personal improvement.

Value of determination and courage
There is a common thread about the importance of courage and determination. Whether it is continuing despite failures, tackling impossible tasks, or embracing radical ideas, they all underscore the need for inner strength.

Focus on impact and value
These quotes suggest that success is not just about personal gain but about creating value and impact. They encourage a shift from seeking mere success to creating something of lasting value.

Transformation and change
Each quote implies a sense of transformation, be it personal, social, or global. They highlight the power of individuals to enact change and the impact one can have on the world.

I found myself pondering whether I could incorporate these concepts into my own field, environment, and ecosystem and begin to communicate and behave in a manner that reflects these ideas, as they profoundly resonated with me.

Therefore, I concentrated on embodying the traits of leaders who inspired me, striving daily to improve these qualities through my actions and words.

In this ever-evolving landscape, resilience has been a cornerstone of my philosophy. Emulating the tenacity of leaders like Churchill and Mandela, I have consistently encouraged my team to view challenges not as setbacks but as opportunities for growth and learning. This mindset has been crucial in a field where technological disruptions and project uncertainties are commonplace. I have found that acknowledging the efforts of the team, even in failure, fosters a culture where taking calculated risks is valued, and learning from mistakes is seen as a path to innovation.

Understanding the diverse motivations of my team has also been key. Some work for financial gain, others for the love of innovation, and many for the sense of community and belonging. To address these varied incentives, I have adopted a multifaceted approach. For those driven by monetary rewards, I ensure fair and transparent compensation structures. For the innovators, I create opportunities for creative freedom and innovative projects. For learners, I focus on continuous skill development and knowledge-sharing sessions. For those seeking community and purpose, I emphasize the broader impact of our work and foster a sense of belonging through virtual team-building activities and open communication platforms.

I recommend that you identify individuals, their actions, or quotes that inspire you. Discover the common elements in these inspirations and diligently work on incorporating them into your own leadership style. By doing so, you can effectively demonstrate these traits to your teams through both your actions and words, fostering an environment of continuous growth and inspiration.

"You can waste your lives drawing lines. Or you can live your life crossing them."
Shonda Rhimes

Operational and Tactical Management

In the dynamic world of managing remote and gig workers, the focus on operational and tactical management is key. This domain explores the practicalities and strategies that are essential for effective management in a decentralized work environment. It is about selecting the right individuals to co-lead or manage diverse teams, ensuring that decision-making processes are inclusive, and adapting working hours to accommodate different time zones. A crucial aspect is the proactive adjustment of pay rates, which reflects the need for flexibility and fairness in compensation. Together, these components create a framework that is not only efficient but also responsive to the unique needs and dynamics of remote teams. Operational and tactical management, therefore, becomes a key driver in sustaining productivity, fostering collaboration, and ensuring the well-being of team members, making it a vital element in the successful management of unknown teams.

1. Selecting the right profiles to co-lead or manage

In a sprawling organization with over a thousand members, primarily consisting of freelancers and gig workers, all operating remotely across various geographies, the dynamics of leadership are significantly amplified. Central to this organization is a leader whose care for the team and dedication to a shared purpose is the driving force behind the culture. However, the sheer scale and diversity of such an organization make it impractical, if not impossible, for a single leader to directly manage every facet and individual. This is where the role of middle management, or more aptly, middle leadership, becomes not just relevant but critically essential.

The importance of middle managers (leaders) aligning with the leader's vision, values, and style cannot be overstated. When there is a disconnect between the leadership demonstrated by the organization's head and the management style practiced by middle managers, the impact can be detrimental. In my own experience leading global organizations, I have seen how misalignment at the middle management level can substantially undermine the integrity and effectiveness of leadership. Middle managers who do not embody the leadership style, which is to lead with care and empathy, but instead operate from a place of ego can disrupt the entire organizational ethos.

The challenge, then, lies in the selection, cultivation, and ongoing development of these middle managers (leaders). A leader who genuinely cares must be thoroughly intentional and strategic in this process. It is crucial to identify individuals who are not only competent in their managerial skills but also deeply resonate with the organization's purpose. These middle managers (leaders) need to be reflections of the leader's principles, living and breathing the organization's purpose in their day-to-day leadership and interactions with their teams.

Often, the pitfall in many organizations is the presence of middle managers who adopt an egocentric, authoritative management style. This approach, especially in a remote, gig-based work environment, is not just ineffective; it is fundamentally damaging. It creates a disconnect between the workforce and the leadership, leading to a breakdown in trust, motivation, and collective purpose. In several instances, I have had to make the difficult decision to transition such managers out of the organization, as their methods were starkly at odds with the values and leadership approach critical for the organization's collective success and well-being.

In extending this discourse, it is imperative to discuss the role of a leader in cultivating middle managers (leaders) who can act as true extensions of their leadership philosophy. This involves more than just selecting the right people; it requires ongoing mentorship, open communication, and a supportive environment where middle managers (leaders) are encouraged to grow and align with the organization's leadership style. Regular training sessions, leadership workshops, and open forums for discussion can be instrumental in nurturing a leadership culture that permeates through all levels of management (leadership).

Furthermore, the leader must establish clear expectations and a framework within which middle managers (leaders) operate. This includes not only goals and targets but also the principles and values that should guide their decision-making and interactions. Periodic reviews and feedback sessions are essential in ensuring that these middle managers (leaders) stay aligned with the organization's purpose and leadership style.

For a leader in a remote, gig-based organization, the meticulous selection and nurturing of middle managers (leaders) is a task of immense importance. These individuals must be more than just overseers or taskmasters; they must be true leaders who mirror the caring, empathetic, and purpose-driven principles of the organization. Ensuring this deep-seated alignment across all levels of leadership is critical for sustaining a healthy, positive organizational culture, fostering trust and motivation among the workforce, and driving the organization toward its collective goals.

Many companies transitioning to remote work during the COVID-19 pandemic faced challenges due to misaligned middle management. In some cases, managers accustomed to traditional, in-person oversight struggled to adapt to remote management, leading to micromanagement, poor communication, and a lack of trust. This not only affected employee morale and productivity but also hindered the organization's overall effectiveness in a remote environment.

Drawing from my own professional journey, I have come to understand the pivotal role of selecting appropriate middle managers (leaders). It is with this insight that I wish to share a story, one that I trust will provoke thoughtful reflection among the readers, encouraging them to contemplate the nuanced art of leadership selection.

Echoes of dissonance

The following is a true story reflected with fictitious names to protect the privacy of the organization and the people involved.

In the sprawling digital landscape, a remote technical consultancy firm known as "Random Consultancy Solutions" thrived. Random Consultancy Solutions, renowned for its innovative approach and global clientele, was led by a charismatic and genuinely caring leader, Elena Martinez. Elena's leadership style was marked by empathy, foresight, and a deep commitment to both her clients and her team. Under her guidance, Random Consultancy Solutions grew exponentially, becoming a reference in remote technical services delivery.

The early days of Random Consultancy Solutions were proof of Elena's ability to handpick middle leadership who shared her vision. These leaders were adept at managing remote teams, fostering a culture of trust, and driving customer satisfaction through exemplary service. Random Consultancy Solutions was not just a company; it was a community bound by shared values and a commitment to excellence.

However, as the pandemic surged, bringing an unprecedented demand for remote technical services, Random Consultancy Solutions faced a new challenge: rapid expansion. The need to scale up quickly was imperative to meet the burgeoning demand. Elena, though astute, found herself in uncharted waters, relying on her trusted middle managers to build out their teams swiftly.

In the haste to expand, a crucial element was overlooked: the careful selection of new middle management. The new managers, brought on board due to urgency rather than a thorough vetting process, did not embody the core values that Elena and her original team cherished. These new managers, driven by ego and a penchant for micromanagement, started creating ripples of discord in the smooth-running Random Consultancy Solutions machinery.

The impact of this misaligned management was not immediate but gradually became evident. Customer satisfaction, once the pride of Random Consultancy Solutions, began to dwindle. Reports of missed deadlines, inadequate consultancy services, and a general sense of dissatisfaction began to emerge. Internally, the once cohesive and enthusiastic Random Consultancy Solutions workforce started showing signs of strain. The new middle managers, more concerned with their own power and control than team well-being or customer satisfaction, instituted rigid protocols and oversight. This shift led to a stifling work environment, sapping the creativity and motivation of the team.

Ethical breaches began to surface, shortcuts were taken to meet unrealistic targets set by the new managers, confidential client information was handled carelessly, and there was a general decline in the integrity of work. The values that Elena had painstakingly instilled in the company were being eroded.

The situation reached a tipping point when a major client threatened to pull out, citing consistent underperformance and a lack of the innovative solutions that Random Consultancy Solutions was once known for. This was a wake-up call for Elena.

She realized that in the quest to scale, the essence of what made Random Consultancy Solutions successful, its people-centric leadership and value-driven approach, had been compromised.

Confronted with this stark reality, Elena took decisive action. She embarked on a rigorous review of her leadership team, re-evaluating the recently appointed middle managers. Those who did not align with the foundational values of Random Consultancy Solutions were transitioned out. She reinstated the thorough vetting process for leadership roles, emphasizing the importance of alignment with the company's core values. Additionally, Elena launched a series of workshops and team-building exercises aimed at rekindling the original spirit of Random Consultancy Solutions.

The road to recovery was not easy, but Elena's commitment to her original vision and her genuine care for her team and clients steered Random Consultancy Solutions back on course. The company emerged stronger, with renewed focus and a reinvigorated team, ready to face the challenges of the ever-evolving digital world.

Random Consultancy Solutions' story serves as a cautionary tale of how rapid growth, if not managed with a steadfast adherence to core values, can lead to a divergence from the very principles that ensure success.

In this context, a leader's foresight in nurturing a pipeline of empathetic middle leaders and the next leaders to replace the current one becomes a strategic imperative. It is about creating a legacy of care that transcends individual tenures and endures as a core organizational value. This approach ensures that the departure of a leader does not create a vacuum in the principles of the organization. Instead, it guarantees the continuity of a culture where every team member feels genuinely supported and valued, irrespective of their role or location.

2. Inclusiveness in decision making

Leading a vast organization, particularly one with a considerable number of remote workers and gig-freelancers, presents unique challenges in maintaining a sense of connection and value among the workforces. While you may not have personal interactions with many of the workers in such a large and diverse group, building connections through genuine care and open conversations is pivotal. Even in an environment where many do not directly belong to your organization, the fundamental human desire for recognition remains universal.

One of the most straightforward yet profoundly impactful ways to make someone feel valued is by soliciting their opinion on decisions. This approach is surprisingly simple yet often overlooked in management practices. Imagine the profound impact on an individual, particularly a remote worker or a freelancer, who might feel detached from the core of the organization when their opinion is earnestly sought on significant matters. It is a gesture that says, "You matter, your thoughts are important, and you are a valued part of this team."

This method goes beyond mere acknowledgment; it fosters a sense of belonging and investment in the organization's goals and decisions. When leaders ask for input, it is not just about gathering diverse perspectives. It is a powerful statement of respect and trust in their team's expertise and judgment. This can be more motivating and affirming than monetary bonuses. Monetary rewards are important, but the emotional and professional satisfaction that comes from being heard and respected can have a longer-lasting impact on an individual's engagement and loyalty.

In my own leadership journey, I have consistently found that involving team members in decision-making processes yields more positive and enthusiastic feedback than sporadic financial incentives. When people feel they are part of the bigger picture and their contributions are making a real difference, it enhances their commitment and satisfaction. This inclusive approach not only enriches the decision-making process with a variety of perspectives but also reinforces a culture of mutual respect and collaboration.

Ultimately, fostering a culture where every voice is valued, especially in a diverse and dispersed workforce, is crucial for sustained engagement and organizational success. It is a strategy that not only nurtures a more inclusive and dynamic workplace but also drives innovation and better decision-making, benefiting the organization.

Now let's look at the power of inclusivity in decision-making from a psychological perspective so you can understand the importance of this leadership practice:

The importance of inclusive decision-making processes cannot be overstated in the constantly changing landscape of modern organizations, particularly those dealing with the complex dynamics of remote and gig-centric workforces. At the heart of this approach lies a fundamental understanding of human psychology and the profound impact that feeling valued has on individuals within a group or organization. At its core, the practice of asking for opinions from team members is not merely a procedural formality but a powerful tool that taps into deep-seated psychological needs and desires. The act of asking for input goes beyond the surface level of gathering diverse ideas; it fosters a sense of belonging and significance among team members. This sentiment is crucial in remote and freelancing environments where physical disconnection can often lead to a sense of isolation or detachment.

From a psychological standpoint, being asked for an opinion triggers a sense of validation in individuals. It communicates that their thoughts and experiences are not only acknowledged but also valued. This validation is a cornerstone of building self-esteem and a sense of competence. When leaders actively seek input, they are indirectly bolstering the self-worth of their team members, leading to increased motivation and engagement. When someone is asked for their opinion in a setting where they perceive themselves as valued, it can set off a symphony within the brain, harmonizing hormones and neurotransmitters to a tune of appreciation and reward. This interaction is a subtle yet profound affirmation, engaging regions of the brain such as the prefrontal cortex and the ventral striatum, which oversee social cognition and the sensation of reward.

This external gesture of seeking one's opinion can prompt an internal release of dopamine, the neurotransmitter that orchestrates the reward circuitry of the brain. The presence of dopamine is like a natural applause, a standing ovation within, signaling feelings of pleasure and contentment. This chemical is a part of the brain's intrinsic reward system that endorses behaviors perceived as positive, reinforcing the desire for similar future interactions.

Concurrently, such recognition may stimulate the secretion of oxytocin, known colloquially as the "bonding hormone." Oxytocin enhances the feeling of trust and strengthens social bonds in interactions. It plays a pivotal role in social engagement and the formation of trust, and a surge of this hormone can intensify feelings of connectedness and trust with others. Additionally, this positive social exchange can manifest in a decrease in cortisol levels, the hormone associated with stress, which is indicative of a relaxed state, contributing to overall health and well-being.

This neurochemical choreography not only generates a sense of well-being but also fosters further social interactions and collaborative behaviors. It reinforces social cohesion and the intrinsic human need to feel recognized and valued within the social fabric.

Moreover, inclusive decision-making processes resonate with the fundamental human need for autonomy. Autonomy, a critical component of self-determination theory, speaks to our inherent desire to have control over our lives and decisions. By involving team members in decision-making, leaders are empowering them, giving them a sense of control and ownership over their work and environment. This empowerment is particularly potent in gig-freelance settings where individuals often seek flexibility and autonomy.

The psychological benefits of inclusive decision-making also extend to the domain of social connectivity. Humans are inherently social beings, and our sense of connection to others plays a pivotal role in our overall mental well-being. Inclusive practices help forge stronger bonds between team members and leaders, fostering a sense of community and shared purpose. In remote work settings, where physical interaction is limited, these social connections become even more vital, serving as a lifeline that bridges the physical gaps. Additionally, involving team members in decision-making processes can lead to better organizational outcomes. Diverse perspectives lead to a richer pool of ideas, fostering innovation and creative problem-solving. When individuals from diverse backgrounds and with different skill sets contribute their viewpoints, the organization benefits from a holistic understanding of challenges and a more robust array of potential solutions.

It is also important to consider the psychological impact of not being included in decision-making. Feelings of exclusion can lead to a sense of alienation, reduced job satisfaction, and diminished loyalty to the organization. In extreme cases, it can even lead to increased turnover as individuals seek environments where they feel more valued and heard.

The practice of seeking and valuing team members' opinions in decision-making processes is much more than a leadership tactic; it is a fundamental approach that aligns with deep-rooted psychological needs for validation, autonomy, and social connectivity. This approach is especially pertinent in the context of remote and freelance workforces, where physical disconnection heightens the need for psychological and emotional connections. By embracing inclusiveness in decision-making, leaders can foster a more engaged, motivated, and cohesive workforce, ultimately driving both individual and organizational success.

Silent meetings

In environments rich with diversity, the challenge of inclusive decision-making becomes particularly pronounced. Even under the guidance of an effective leader or manager who fosters participation in decision-making processes, the dynamics of a diverse team in a physical meeting room can skew towards the voices of the more vocal individuals. This often leaves those with more reserved dispositions feeling unable to contribute meaningfully to decisions. Now, transpose this scenario to a remote setup, or even more complex, within a gig-freelance ecosystem, and the challenge magnifies.

Drawing from my own experiences, we have encountered this hurdle numerous times. Despite our best efforts in facilitating inclusive discussions, feedback consistently highlighted a common issue: meetings being dominated by the more outspoken members, overshadowing the quieter voices in sessions meant for collective decision-making. Even with a leader's adept orchestration, ensuring equitable participation in these scenarios is a formidable task.

The solution, however, emerged from learning through our missteps and harnessing the power of feedback. We introduced the silent meeting concept in scenarios demanding decisions that require inclusive input from all team members. This approach revolutionizes the traditional meeting format, especially in the remote and gig-freelance contexts, by creating a more balanced platform for every voice to be heard and considered, thus fostering a truly inclusive decision-making environment.

If you have never heard about the silent meeting concept, here is a summary of how it was born, how it works, and its extensive benefits:

Silent meetings, a concept as revolutionary as it is simple, emerged from the pressing need to redefine the dynamics of group discussions in our increasingly diverse and remote work environments. This innovative approach was born out of the recognition that traditional meetings, despite their intentions, often fall short of harnessing the full spectrum of perspectives within a team. The louder voices tend to dominate, while the more reserved yet equally insightful members recede into the background. In a world where collaboration is key, this imbalance needed redressal, and thus, the silent meeting emerged as a solution. At the heart of a silent meeting is the idea of leveling the playing field. It operates on a simple yet effective premise: every participant, irrespective of their disposition, gets an equal opportunity to contribute without the pressure of vocal competition. This method particularly shines in remote or gig-freelance setups, where the nuances of physical presence are absent, and the challenge of ensuring equitable participation becomes even more pronounced.

How it works is both straightforward and ingenious. In a silent meeting, the agenda and discussion points are shared in advance. Participants prepare their input, often in written form, which is then consolidated and shared with the group. The meeting itself is conducted with minimal verbal discussion. Instead, members review the collective input silently, making notes or annotations.

After this phase, the next step typically involves a more interactive segment. Here, participants can share their thoughts, either verbally or in written form, based on the notes and annotations made during the silent review. This part of the meeting is structured to ensure that each participant's insights are considered and discussed. The facilitator or leader of the meeting plays a crucial role in this stage. They might guide the conversation by highlighting key points or questions that arose during the silent review. Alternatively, they could invite participants to expand on their written comments, ensuring that those who are less vocal have the same opportunity to contribute as those who are more outspoken. This interactive phase is designed to foster a deeper understanding of the diverse perspectives and ideas that have been presented. It encourages collaboration and problem-solving, as participants can now engage in discussions that are informed by the collective insights gathered during the silent part of the meeting. The goal is to reach a consensus or at least have a clear understanding of the various viewpoints. This process helps in making informed decisions that reflect the collective wisdom and input of the entire group. By incorporating both silent and interactive elements, the meeting format aims to balance inclusivity and efficiency, ensuring that all voices are heard and valued in the decision-making process. This approach not only levels the playing field for the introverted and extroverted alike but also fosters deeper, more thoughtful engagement with the content.

Companies that have embraced this concept report a multitude of benefits. For starters, it democratizes the decision-making process. Every team member, regardless of their rank or personality type, gets a voice. This inclusivity leads to more diverse perspectives being brought to the table, enriching the decision-making process. Additionally, silent meetings are often more efficient. Without the usual back-and-forth of conventional meetings, they tend to be more focused, leading to quicker, more effective decision-making.

The silent meeting also champions a more thoughtful and reflective approach to collaboration. Without the pressure to respond immediately, participants can digest information more thoroughly, leading to more considered and nuanced contributions. This is particularly beneficial in complex or sensitive discussions where the immediate reactions can be less insightful or even counterproductive.

Companies advocating silent meetings note an improvement in the overall meeting culture. The approach reduces meeting fatigue, a common ailment in today's corporate world, by making meetings more purposeful and less frequent. When meetings are more about thoughtful contribution and less about immediate reaction, the need for constant meetings diminishes.

The silent meeting is not just a meeting format; it is a cultural shift. It represents a move towards more thoughtful, inclusive, and efficient ways of working together. By giving equal weight to all voices, regardless of their volume, silent meetings are paving the way for a more equitable and effective future in business communication and decision-making. As we continue to go through the complexities of modern work environments, especially in remote and freelance settings, the silent meeting is proof of the power of quiet, reflective collaboration.

In my professional experience, the concept of silent meetings has undergone a subtle yet significant evolution, all while staying true to its original principle. This evolution has been instrumental in refining the process of silent meetings, which we have orchestrated with great care. Here is how the process unfolds:

Setting the stage

The lead initiates the process by distributing key documents and resources pertinent to the decision-making topic. This early step is crucial in laying a solid foundation for an inclusive and well-informed discussion.

Collaborative platform

A Microsoft Word document is shared in advance with all participants via a cloud location, enabling simultaneous contributions from everyone. This document acts as a dynamic, collaborative platform, allowing everyone to contribute their thoughts online simultaneously, fostering a sense of collective engagement.

Asynchronous contribution

Participants are encouraged to add their comments, data points, arguments, and insights at their own pace. The process is designed to accommodate different schedules, allowing contributions both before and during the silent meeting, ensuring flexibility and inclusiveness.

Meeting commencement

As the silent meeting begins, the leader succinctly outlines the purpose and desired outcomes, focusing on the nature of input expected. While keeping computer cameras on is preferred to foster a sense of connection, participants have the freedom to turn them off, catering to individual comfort levels.

Engagement and dialogue

The core of the meeting revolves around participants engaging with the content in the shared document. They delve into each other's comments, enriching the discussion with questions, challenges, or additional data. The use of visual aids like labels, pictures, icons, and various fonts adds depth and clarity to communication.

Wordless interaction

As the meeting progresses, a rich variation of silent dialogue evolves within the document. Participants freely express their opinions, emotions, and potential solutions, all articulated without speaking a single word, embodying the essence of silent communication.

Consolidation of insights

Post meeting, the leader takes on the crucial role of consolidating all the inputs gathered. This step might involve a follow-up session for clarifications, ensuring that every contribution is considered and valued.

Decision making

The culmination of this process is a decision often made in a subsequent short meeting. This decision reflects the collaborative effort and diverse perspectives of the team, underlining the inclusive nature of this approach.

The beauty of this refined silent meeting process lies in its ability to maintain the spirit of its original intent while enhancing the collaborative and inclusive nature of decision making in a diverse work environment. Everyone's voice is heard and considered. It is evidence of the evolving nature of workplace communication and teamwork, adapting to the nuances and needs of modern work settings.

3. Adjusting your working time to others

Leading a remote organization, especially one that includes gig workers or freelancers, poses unique challenges, the most important among them being the coordination of disparate time zones and working hours. In my career, a persistent issue has been the disparity between my time zone and working hours and those of the management or leadership team. Often, it seemed that the working hours of the leadership team were untouchable, with meetings and engagements rigidly confined within their time zone. This inflexibility often left many unable to participate without compromising their personal schedules or family time.

The pursuit of work-life balance is undoubtedly important, and every individual's need for this balance should be respected. However, leading an organization with care demands more than just respecting your own time; it requires a willingness to adapt and align with others' schedules. This flexibility is not just a courtesy but a cornerstone of effective leadership in a remote setting.

When we lead by example, showing a readiness to adjust our schedules, we are not just accommodating others; we are actively demonstrating a culture of respect and equality. True leadership is about finding a balance between meeting organizational needs and respecting the individual circumstances of team members. It is about understanding that in a remote work environment, everyone's time is valuable and deserves equal consideration.

Flexibility in scheduling is a two-way street. While there may be occasions when team members need to align with the leader's schedule, it is equally important for leaders to reciprocate. This approach fosters a sense of mutual respect and understanding, which is crucial in a remote work environment where physical presence is replaced by digital communication. Moreover, this flexibility is not just beneficial for employee morale; it also has practical advantages. By accommodating various time zones and schedules, leaders can tap into a diverse range of perspectives and insights, enhancing the decision-making process and fostering a more inclusive work environment. It also sends a clear message: that every team member, regardless of their location or working hours, is an integral part of the organization.

Leading a remote organization requires a paradigm shift in how we view time and availability. It is about transcending traditional office hours and embracing a global mindset where inclusivity and flexibility are not just appreciated but are integral to the organization's DNA. By doing so, leaders not only build a more cohesive and motivated team but also lay the groundwork for a more dynamic, responsive, and ultimately successful organization.

In the contemporary arena of global business, where the confines of traditional office hours and geographical boundaries have become increasingly blurred, the sensitivity of leaders to the varied time zones of their teams has emerged as a crucial facet of effective leadership. In my own experience, I find it imperative to explore the repercussions of managerial indifference to time zone differences, particularly regarding its impact on employee engagement, increased workload, and organizational retention.

The essence of employee engagement, a vital component in the machinery of organizational psychology, hinges significantly on the perception of being valued and respected. When managers overlook the time zone differences of their team members, they inadvertently project a message of disregard, leading to feelings of alienation and a sense that the individual's personal time is undervalued. This lack of acknowledgment, especially in a global team, can precipitate a decline in morale and engagement levels.

Beyond the psychological impact, practical consequences also surface. A manager's failure to account for time zone disparities can lead to scheduling conflicts, increased fatigue due to irregular working hours, and a resultant drop in productivity. Employees compelled to catch up on missed calls or meetings outside their standard working hours find themselves burdened with an additional workload. This not only exacerbates their daily tasks but can also lead to miscommunications and errors, hampering overall efficiency.

From a human resources perspective, the health of an organization is closely tied to its employee turnover rates. When employees consistently need to compromise their personal time due to managerial insensitivity to time zones, it breeds dissatisfaction and disengagement. In an era where the workforce increasingly prioritizes flexibility and work-life balance, such discontent can drive valuable talent to seek organizations that offer more empathetic and adaptable management approaches.

Leadership, in its true essence, is about adapting to the needs of those being led. In our interconnected world, this adaptation extends to respecting and accommodating the diverse time zones of a global team. A leader's failure to demonstrate this understanding can create a disconnect between employees and leadership, undermining the effectiveness of remote collaboration.

The issue of managers disregarding employee time zones is far from trivial. Its implications span the spectrum from individual employee engagement to broader operational efficiency and overall health of an organization.

As businesses continue to navigate the complexities of global operations, the need for sensitive and adaptable leadership becomes ever more pronounced. In today's workspace, respecting and considering the time constraints of a diverse team is not just a courtesy but an essential attribute of effective and empathetic leadership.

To address the challenges posed by varying time zones and working hours, I implemented several strategies. These not only catered to my own time zone and work schedule but also aimed to maintain engagement and connection while respecting the work-life balance of my team members. The following practices were particularly effective:

Rotating round-the-clock one-to-one and team meetings

To ensure everyone has a fair share of convenience, I rotate meeting times, especially if those are one-to-one meetings with workers, regardless of their roles. This approach brings a democratic balance that everyone really appreciates. Each team member experiences both the convenience of a meeting in their daytime and the commitment of an occasional late night or early morning call.

Virtual office hours

I set up "open hours" during which I am accessible for a specific duration, allowing team members from all time zones to join in for discussions or casual catchups. These slots can be reserved by individuals or groups. To cater to all workers, I schedule these open hours at various times throughout the week, including weekends.

Flexibility to changes

I foster a flexible and understanding work environment where last-minute alterations to meeting schedules are not viewed as inconveniences. This approach ensures that team members do not feel any undue guilt or stress if they need to adjust meeting days or times. The emphasis is on open communication and mutual respect, which allows for such changes to be accommodated seamlessly. This way, everyone can focus on their work and personal life without worrying about rigid schedules, thus promoting a healthy work-life balance.

In conclusion, managing a global team across different time zones and work schedules requires a blend of creativity, flexibility, and respect for individual needs. The practices I implemented ensure that every team member, regardless of their role or location, feels valued and heard. They foster a democratic balance that is appreciated by all, demonstrating that with the right approach, it is possible to navigate the complexities of a global 24/7 work environment while respecting everyone's time and personal life.

4. Proactive rate adjustments

Studies based on surveys state that while Baby Boomers value job security and a steady career trajectory, often avoiding risks and new technologies, Generation X tends to prioritize work-life balance and flexibility, showing a preference for independence and self-reliance. Millennials, on the other hand, seek meaningful work that offers a sense of purpose, gender equality, and inclusive benefits, along with flexible post-pandemic work arrangements and safe, participatory work environments. The newest to the workforce, Generation Z, values financial compensation with pay transparency, open communication, control over their work lives, social support at work, a focus on mental health and well-being, opportunities for growth and feedback, and work that aligns with a strong sense of purpose and personal mission, particularly in addressing social issues.

Let's face a candid reality: income is essential for ensuring the well-being and stability of ourselves and our families, no matter which generation we belong to. Throughout my career, I've yet to encounter someone who loves their job to the extent of working without pay. It is reasonable to assume that individuals who might do so are those who have secured not only their financial future but those of several generations to come.

In the scope of gig-freelance and remote work, the significance of monetary compensation in shaping worker satisfaction and retention cannot be underestimated. While factors such as job purpose, flexibility, and autonomy play a crucial role in motivating today's workforce, the foundational aspect of financial reward stands as a cornerstone in the employer-employee relationship.

Organizations typically conduct salary or rate reviews during specific periods, but these practices vary widely. Some align salary increases with yearly inflation, a practice that maintains the purchasing power of employees in a fluctuating economy. Inflation rates, however, are not uniform across regions. For instance, countries experiencing hyperinflation require more frequent salary adjustments to retain staff effectively. Countries like Venezuela and Zimbabwe have faced extreme inflation rates, requiring a more dynamic approach to compensation.

Performance-based salary increases are another common method. This approach, rooted in meritocracy, rewards employees for achieving certain benchmarks or exceeding expectations. However, performance metrics can be subjective and may not always accurately reflect an employee's contribution, especially in roles where output is harder to quantify.

On the other end of the spectrum, there are instances where companies do not routinely adjust wages. This can lead to a decline in employee morale and productivity as workers feel undervalued. Many studies state that salary is an important factor influencing job satisfaction and turnover.

Counteroffers are also a significant part of the compensation landscape. They are often used as a retention strategy for key employees considering leaving. While effective in the short term, employees who accept counteroffers are likely to leave the company within a year, suggesting that factors beyond salary contribute to their initial dissatisfaction.

The concept of "money doesn't matter" is increasingly being challenged in today's work environment. My research shows that fair wages play a crucial role in enhancing job satisfaction and maintaining employee loyalty. Workers need to feel that their compensation reflects their effort and skills. Moreover, organizations need to consider external economic conditions, like cost of living and inflation, alongside internal factors, like performance and role importance, in their compensation strategies. This comprehensive approach ensures that employees feel genuinely valued, not just in words or through recognition programs but in tangible financial terms. While intrinsic motivators like purpose and job satisfaction are important, they cannot replace the fundamental need for fair and competitive compensation. A holistic approach that combines both financial and non-financial incentives is key to fostering a motivated and committed workforce.

Drawing on my extensive experience, I have witnessed firsthand how economic conditions significantly influence worker satisfaction and organizational success. In the organizations I have been leading, we have consistently factored in these considerations, ensuring that our approach holistically addresses the multifaceted needs of our workforce. This strategy has proven effective, yielding remarkable results not only in terms of employee fulfillment but also in enhancing individual and organizational productivity.

A key outcome of this approach is the noticeable improvement in our organization's reputation. We have become a sought-after workplace where potential workforce are keen to join, knowing they will be part of an excellently managed team where their contributions are both recognized and rewarded. This reputation extends beyond mere leadership; it encompasses a culture where individuals can truly thrive, showcasing their best selves. Our focus on valuing our workforce both socially and economically has established a standard of care and respect that resonates deeply with them. This balance of professional fulfillment and financial recognition creates an environment where everyone feels genuinely appreciated and motivated, driving the organization toward sustained success and growth.

The gig and freelance economy brings unique challenges and opportunities, especially concerning the retention and remuneration of workers. One vital factor to bear in mind is the relative simplicity for gig workers and freelancers to leave an organization compared to their full-time counterparts, particularly in situations of insufficient compensation.

For freelancers and gig workers, the decision to leave a project or an organization is often straightforward and can be made with relative ease. This flexibility is primarily due to the nature of their contracts, which are typically short-term and project-based. Unlike full-time employees bound by more rigid contractual obligations and processes, gig workers operate with a greater sense of autonomy and independence. Their engagement with an organization is often transactional and focused on specific deliverables, making it easier for them to move on to other opportunities if they feel undercompensated or undervalued.

In contrast, full-time employees are more deeply entrenched in the organizations they work for. They often have long-term contracts, enjoy benefits like health insurance and retirement plans, and are integrated into the company culture. Leaving a full-time position usually involves a more complex process, including notice periods, exit interviews, and the potential loss of long-term benefits. This complexity can sometimes dissuade full-time employees from leaving a job, even when they are dissatisfied with the monetary compensation they receive.

Given the ease with which gig workers can leave, it is crucial for organizations to proactively and adequately compensate these individuals, especially those delivering exceptional work within the gig-freelancing space. Gig workers who consistently produce high-quality outcomes are invaluable assets, and their departure can lead to significant disruptions in operations, loss of specialized skills, and additional costs associated with finding and onboarding new talent.

In the gig economy, reputation matters immensely. Freelancers and gig workers often share their experiences with peers and on public platforms. An organization known for underpaying risks damaging its reputation, making it harder to attract top-tier talent in the future.

The gig-freelancer workforce is often the bearer of specialized skills and display a remarkable ability to adapt swiftly to various projects. The agility and expertise they bring to the table are not easily replaceable, making their loss a challenging and time-intensive setback for any organization. Similarly, the gig-freelancer workforce is frequently involved in critical projects that come with tight deadlines, and their abrupt departure can significantly disrupt project timelines, leading to a drop in overall productivity. When it comes to recruitment, the process of finding and integrating new freelancers who can perform at a high level from the outset often entails a substantial investment in both time and resources, sometimes even more so than hiring a full-time employee. Furthermore, while they may not be as deeply integrated as their full-time counterparts, experienced freelancers gather a wealth of institutional knowledge, which is a loss to the organization when they move on.

As the gig and freelance economy continues to expand, it becomes increasingly important for organizations to understand and appreciate the unique dynamics of working with these professionals. Ensuring that freelancers are compensated fairly and competitively is not merely a question of fairness; it is a critical strategic decision. By investing in the satisfaction of gig workers, organizations can foster long-lasting relationships, ensure continuity of high-quality work, and maintain a formidable reputation in the competitive freelance market. Neglecting these considerations can lead to losses that surpass mere financial figures, potentially compromising the very operational efficiency and structural integrity of the organization.

"There is no magic formula for great company culture. The key is just to treat your staff how you would like to be treated."
Richard Branson

Organizational Structure and Culture

This section is crucial in shaping the environment of teams, particularly in the remote and gig economy context. This section dives into how organizational design and cultural attributes impact team dynamics and effectiveness. It explores the importance of a flat organizational hierarchy, fostering a servant mindset among leaders, and addressing challenges like accommodating loneliness in remote work settings. These aspects are key to building a supportive and efficient work culture. As we move forward, we will explore the nuances of a flat organization, the philosophy behind a servant mindset, and strategies for accommodating loneliness, each contributing to the foundation of a strong, cohesive organizational culture.

1. An emblem reflecting identity

Emblems and flags have always fascinated me, as they are powerful symbols representing the identity of various groups. Their role in our collective history is significant and captivating. These symbols often unify people from different backgrounds or serve practical purposes, like in ancient battlefields where they helped identify soldiers and allies. Research confirms that flags and emblems symbolize unity and common causes. In organizational contexts, they are instrumental in fostering a sense of collective identity among diverse groups. This is particularly relevant in our organization, where we strive to create a shared sense of belonging regardless of our team's diversity.

In my career, marked by managing various programs with diverse workforces, my first consistent action when starting to create or lead a team was to establish a unifying community name, augmented by a unique emblem. This practice was particularly pivotal in large, geographically dispersed organizations, which often consisted of numerous smaller sub-groups, whether they were teams or sub-organizations. Each of these smaller entities, I observed, greatly benefited from having their own unique identity and emblem. This approach fostered a sense of belonging and pride among the members. During my tenure, I have seen the amazing creativity of these teams manifest in various forms. Remarkably, some teams went beyond merely creating logos. I recall one team that went as far as designing their own flag. Another team composed an anthem that poignantly encapsulated their shared values and principles. Many teams designed t-shirts and distributed them amongst the team members, and they joined virtual meetings with those t-shirts.

What stood out in these initiatives was the profound impact they had in forging connections among team members, particularly in environments where physical interaction was minimal or non-existent, such as in fully remote settings or in scenarios involving gig workers and freelancers. These symbols and anthems served as tangible representations of their collective spirit and goals, transcending the limitations of physical distance. These unique identifiers played a crucial role in fostering a sense of competition and camaraderie. In large organizations, where individual contributions can sometimes feel diluted, having a distinct team identity helps in recognizing and celebrating the achievements of each group. This, in turn, motivates individuals to contribute more actively towards their team's success.

Furthermore, in a gig economy, where traditional organizational structures are often absent, such emblems and anthems provide a sense of structure and belonging. They help create a more cohesive work environment, which is essential for productivity and job satisfaction in these flexible work arrangements while at the same time addressing loneliness.

My experiences have underscored the importance of these small but significant elements in creating a unified, motivated, and productive workforce, especially in diverse and dispersed organizational structures.

2. A flat organization

I have always been deeply fascinated by the unique and dynamic environments of startup organizations. Their vibrant, innovative culture is captivating, as these smaller-scale entities often foster a collaborative spirit where team members engage in a wide array of tasks and responsibilities. This versatile approach to business has significantly influenced my perspective on organizational models, highlighting the effectiveness of adaptability and team-oriented strategies.

As startups grow and mature, they naturally transition towards more structured hierarchies and formal organizational strategies. This evolution often brings about increased bureaucracy and, unfortunately, can lead to a shift in focus towards internal power dynamics among management. It is a trend I have observed in many of the companies I have had the privilege to work with. This shift often results in a reduction of the collective focus on external challenges and opportunities, leading to internal conflicts that can detract from the company's original mission and goals.

In order to understand the foundations of hugely successful organizational structures, I was delighted to discover a remarkable book written by Frederic Laloux titled *Reinventing Organizations*. This book provides insightful perspectives on how organizations can be structured and managed to achieve both efficiency and a positive, thriving workplace culture. The book was first published in 2014 and has since gained significant attention in business and organizational development communities. The book explores how organizations can evolve beyond their current structures to become more soulful, purposeful, and productive.

Laloux presents a model of organizational development that categorizes organizations into different stages, each characterized by a specific color: Red, Amber, Orange, Green, and Teal.

These colors represent different paradigms and approaches to management and organizational structure:

Red organizations
These organizations operate in a very basic, authoritarian way, similar to tribal structures. They are often characterized by a high degree of chaos and exercise power through fear.

Amber organizations
These are hierarchical and role-oriented organizations that are often found in government agencies, public schools, and the military. They focus on stability, order, and predictability.

Orange organizations
Driven by achievement and success, they are often goal-oriented, focusing on innovation and meritocracy. Many modern corporations fall into this category.

Green organizations
These organizations prioritize values, culture, and empowerment. They focus on stakeholder engagement and have a more egalitarian approach.

Teal organizations
The most advanced in Laloux's model, teal organizations operate with a high degree of autonomy and self-management. They focus on a holistic approach, integrating the needs of the organization with the well-being of its employees.

Laloux argues that teal organizations represent the future of work, emphasizing self-management, wholeness, and a deeper sense of purpose. His ideas have been influential in discussions about how organizations can adapt and thrive in rapidly changing environments. The book provides case studies of organizations that have successfully implemented these principles, offering insights into the challenges and benefits of this transformational approach.

Teal organizations represent the forefront of organizational evolution. They operate based on self-management, empowering individuals rather than enforcing a top-down approach. This model is not just a structure but a mindset that values the whole person, integrating employees' needs and well-being into the organization's fabric.

The benefits of this approach are manifold. Firstly, it fosters a culture of trust and autonomy. In a remote, gig-based setting like ours, where team members are spread across different cultures and technical backgrounds, autonomy is not just beneficial; it is essential. Teal organizations allow individuals to make decisions aligned with their expertise, encouraging innovation and rapid problem-solving.

Teal structures are inherently flexible. In the fast-paced, ever-evolving world of technology, adaptability is key. By decentralizing decision-making and flattening hierarchies, teal organizations can pivot quickly, responding to market changes and technological advancements more effectively.

Perhaps most importantly, teal organizations recognize the human aspect of work. They create spaces where individuals can bring their whole selves to their roles, fostering a sense of purpose and belonging. This aspect is crucial in a gig-freelancer workforce, where isolation and disconnection can be challenges.

As leaders, we need to acknowledge that the shift to teal is not just desirable; it is necessary. The traditional hierarchical organizational models are increasingly incompatible with the dynamic, diverse nature of today's global, remote or gig-based workforce. By embracing the principles of teal organizations, we can create more resilient, innovative, and human-centered workplaces.

Having led a diverse, remote workforce of over a thousand gig-freelancers in the technology sector, I have witnessed firsthand the changing landscape of work. My conviction that the future of work is remote and gig-based grows stronger daily. This belief was further solidified after reading Frederic Laloux's enlightening book *Reinventing Organizations*, which offers a visionary outlook on organizational evolution.

In my experience, many talented individuals are leaving behind traditional hierarchical structures, especially prevalent in less developed countries, seeking respite from rigid, often oppressive, corporate environments. Laloux's book resonates deeply with this shift, outlining a spectrum of organizational models, from the red paradigm of authoritarian control to the groundbreaking teal model.

In the dynamic journey of organizational development, it is often necessary to embrace change at various levels, including leadership. This evolution requires a shift towards inclusivity and openness in management style. As eloquently expressed by Satya Nadella, adopting a learn-it-all mindset is crucial for leaders in contemporary organizations. This approach prioritizes continuous learning, adaptability, and a commitment to collaborative progress over traditional hierarchical power structures.

This transformation in leadership aligns with the principle of fostering an environment where knowledge and innovation are not confined to specific roles but are a collective pursuit. The emphasis is on cultivating leaders who are not just managers in the conventional sense but are visionary facilitators. They are individuals who empower teams, encourage diverse perspectives, and drive the organization forward with a shared vision rather than wielding power in a traditional top-down approach. This progressive perspective on leadership is essential for organizations aiming to stay relevant and thrive in an ever-evolving business landscape.

In my experience leading remote technology organizations, I have always been drawn to innovative models of management and structure. This fascination led me to embrace a non-hierarchical model, a nuanced variation of the teal organization, as described in Laloux's seminal work, *Reinventing Organizations*. This approach has not just been a strategy but a core principle shaping every aspect of my leadership.

At the heart of this non-hierarchical model lies the simple yet profound idea of a flat organizational structure. In the teams I have led, there is no traditional hierarchy. Everyone has a **role**, but these roles do not imply a ladder of authority. As a leader, my primary function is to facilitate the work and outcomes of others, guided always by a principle of care. This approach resonates deeply with the principles of teal organizations, where self-management and holistic engagement are key.

In the organizations I lead, doors are always open, metaphorically speaking in our remote context. I prioritize accessibility and transparency over hierarchy. There is no need for political correctness; instead, we uphold a culture of mutual respect. This openness allows concerns to be unfolded transparently and addressed through constant dialogue. From the smallest team to the largest unit, each operates autonomously yet in alignment with our organizational principles and values.

In the teams I work with, we place a high value on ensuring that every new team member is thoroughly oriented and understands the unique structure and ethos of our workplace. We prioritize a culture of equality and collaborative respect, and it is imperative that all employees are aware of this from the outset.

To maintain this environment, we actively discourage behaviors that emphasize or reinforce traditional hierarchical structures. It is important that our team operates on a foundation of mutual respect and open communication, where the focus is on collective goals rather than individual power dynamics.

Our approach is to nurture a positive and inclusive workplace where everyone's contributions are valued equally. By guiding team members away from actions that might undermine this principle, we are committed to creating a space where everyone can thrive and work together harmoniously toward our shared objectives.

The advantages of this non-hierarchical model are significant, especially in a remote, gig-based workforce. It fosters a culture of trust and empowerment, where individuals are encouraged to take ownership of their work. This autonomy not only drives innovation but also accelerates problem-solving, as decisions are made by those closest to work.

Flexibility is another key feature of this approach. In the fast-paced tech industry, the ability to adapt quickly to new challenges and opportunities is crucial. A flat structure, devoid of cumbersome layers of management, enables us to pivot and respond with agility.

Moreover, this model recognizes and nurtures the human aspect of work. It creates an environment where individuals can bring their whole selves to their roles, fostering not just a sense of belonging but also a deeper connection to work and the organization.

As we look to the future, traditional hierarchical models are becoming increasingly obsolete, especially in a diverse, global, and dynamic industry like technology. The shift towards a non-hierarchical, teal-inspired approach is not just a trend but a necessary evolution. By embracing these principles, we are paving the way for more resilient, innovative, and human-centered workplaces.

3. A servant mindset

Lao Tzu, an ancient Chinese philosopher and writer, once said: "A leader is best when people barely know he exists; when his work is done, his aim fulfilled, they will say: we did it ourselves." This quote subtly captures the essence of servant leadership, emphasizing the idea that the most effective leaders are those who empower their teams to such an extent that the team feels success as their own.

This perspective is especially pertinent in the context of remote or gig work, where the physical distance between leaders and their teams can often translate into a more hands-off management style. By focusing on empowerment and support rather than direct control, a servant leader can inspire a sense of ownership and autonomy in their team. This approach can be incredibly effective in motivating gig workers and freelancers, who often value independence and self-direction. It suggests that the role of the leader is not to be at the forefront but to be the guiding force that enables the team to achieve and recognize their own potential and accomplishments.

Robert K. Greenleaf was a visionary in the field of leadership studies and is best known as the founder of the modern servant leadership movement. Greenleaf embarked on a successful career at AT&T, where he served for 40 years, eventually becoming the director of management research.

After retiring from AT&T in 1964, Greenleaf embarked on a second career that spanned 25 years, during which he made significant contributions as an author, teacher, and consultant. His most influential work is the book *The Servant as Leader*, published in 1970, which introduced the concept of servant leader and laid the foundation for the modern servant leadership movement. This book and his subsequent writings have had a profound impact on leadership theory and practice, emphasizing the importance of leaders serving their teams and communities.

Greenleaf's concept of servant leadership, as outlined in his book *Servant Leadership*, is highly relevant to the corporate world. This leadership style, focused on serving others, contrasts sharply with traditional top-down management approaches. In a corporate setting, servant leadership translates to prioritizing the needs and development of employees, which in turn drives better service, innovation, and business performance. Companies led by servant leaders often foster a culture of empowerment, collaboration, and ethical responsibility. Greenleaf's philosophy suggests that when corporations adopt servant leadership principles, they not only enhance their operational effectiveness but also contribute positively to broader societal well-being. This approach is particularly effective in today's dynamic business environment, where employee engagement and social responsibility are increasingly vital to corporate success.

Throughout my leadership journey, I have encountered a wide spectrum of management styles, some of which starkly contrast with the servant leadership ideals proposed by Greenleaf. I have seen managers who, regrettably, viewed their role as one where they were to be served by their teams. These managers often leveraged their hierarchical power primarily for personal gain, leading to environments where employees felt undervalued and often left at the earliest opportunity. This approach starkly contrasts with true servant leaders I have met, those who see themselves as enablers and supporters of their teams.

These servant leaders dedicate themselves to removing obstacles for their team members, fostering an environment conducive to success and growth. They go beyond mere management; they invest in their team's development, coach them, and advocate for their achievements within the broader organization. This not only amplifies their team's visibility for better professional opportunities but also creates a culture of mutual respect and empowerment.

The dichotomy between a manager who is not a leader and a true leader is profound. While the former operates on a paradigm of self-interest and authority, the latter thrives on empathy, support, and a genuine commitment to the team's well-being and growth. This understanding of the leader's role is pivotal in today's corporate landscape, resonating with Greenleaf's vision of servant leadership, where the leader's success is intrinsically tied to the success of their team members. Such leadership fosters a more engaged, motivated, and loyal workforce, driving both individual and organizational success.

The role of a servant leader takes on new dimensions in remote work or gig-freelancing ecosystems, and this role is defined by a relentless commitment to the growth and success of their team. Servant leaders in this context are more than a figurehead; they become an integral part of the team's journey, proactively removing obstacles, sharing the workload, and leading by example, especially in challenging situations.

Servant leadership, in a remote or gig environment, is characterized by a profound commitment to the team's welfare. Leaders in these settings shoulder the responsibility of ensuring that their team members face minimal barriers in their workflow. This involves understanding the unique challenges of remote work, such as isolation, variable schedules, and the need for flexibility, addressing them with empathy and creativity.

A key aspect of servant leadership is the proactive identification and removal of obstacles that hinder team performance. This could range from addressing technical challenges to ensuring effective communication channels. The leader's role is to anticipate potential issues and address them before they impact the team.

In a remote setup, servant leaders are actively involved in the work itself, willing to roll up their sleeves and contribute alongside their team, and, hence, share the workload. This not only demonstrates commitment but also provides the leader with an intimate understanding of the challenges faced by their team. When situations demand, servant leaders are the first to step into the frontline, leading by example and demonstrating a hands-on approach. This could involve taking the lead on critical projects or stepping in to resolve high-stakes issues. Servant leaders prioritize the professional growth of their team members. They invest time in coaching, providing feedback, and creating opportunities for skill development. This aspect is especially crucial in remote settings, where career development paths might not be as visible or structured.

In remote work environments, building a supportive and inclusive culture is essential. Servant leaders focus on nurturing a sense of community and belonging despite the physical distances. They facilitate regular team interactions and foster an environment where every member feels valued and heard. Leading remotely involves navigating several challenges, such as ensuring consistent engagement, maintaining team cohesion, and effectively managing diverse work styles and schedules. Servant leaders must be adept at using technology to bridge communication gaps and create a sense of proximity. They also need to be flexible, adapting their leadership style to suit the needs of a diverse and distributed team.

As the world leans more towards remote work and gig economies, the qualities of a servant leader become increasingly significant. Such a leadership style is essential for building trust, fostering autonomy, and ensuring elevated levels of engagement in environments where traditional supervisory methods are less effective. By prioritizing the well-being and development of their team, servant leaders create a robust and adaptable workforce, ready to meet the challenges of an evolving work landscape.

The servant leader in a remote or gig-freelancing world embodies a blend of empathy, proactive support, hands-on involvement, and a strong commitment to team development. This leadership style is key to navigating the complexities of modern work environments and unlocking the full potential of remote or gig teams.

4. Accommodating loneliness

The phenomenon of loneliness among remote and gig workers is a growing concern in today's workforce, meriting closer examination from a psychological perspective. The arrival of remote work, accelerated by technological advancements and the global pandemic, has fundamentally altered the traditional workspace. While it offers flexibility and autonomy, it also brings an undercurrent of isolation that can have profound psychological effects on workers, particularly in the gig economy.

From a psychological standpoint, loneliness is not merely the physical absence of others; it is a perceived social isolation, a sense of disconnection from a community, or a lack of a sense of belonging. This feeling can be particularly acute among remote and gig workers who often miss the day-to-day interpersonal interactions and the informal social networks that form in a traditional office environment. The transitory nature of gig work exacerbates this, as workers frequently shift between projects with little opportunity to form lasting relationships with colleagues.

The consequences of this isolation are significant. Loneliness has been linked to a variety of mental health issues, including depression, anxiety, and decreased cognitive function. It can also lead to feelings of decreased self-worth, as workers may feel undervalued or unseen. Furthermore, chronic loneliness is increasingly being recognized as a risk factor for physical health problems comparable to smoking or obesity.

The sporadic and project-based nature of gig work often results in a lack of steady colleagues or team dynamics. This transient professional life means fewer opportunities for deep, meaningful connections, which are crucial for emotional and psychological well-being. Moreover, the competitive and solitary nature of many gig roles can foster a sense of isolation, even when interacting in online environments. Companies and leaders within these sectors face a critical challenge: addressing and mitigating loneliness and its associated consequences among their workforces. This involves creating opportunities for connection and community building, even in a virtual space.

Based on the studies I conducted and the surveys I carried out over the past six years, 40% of gig workers reported feeling lonely in their daily lives, a rate significantly higher than that of traditional full-time employees. However, in our organization, following the implementation of specific measures, only 10% of gig workers reported experiencing loneliness. This demonstrates the positive impact of the concepts and practices we have been sharing and will continue to disseminate, in preventing loneliness among gig workers.

While regular check-ins, virtual team-building activities, and fostering an inclusive culture where every voice is heard can help mitigate feelings of isolation, some additional practices we had, could help overcome loneliness in remote or gig-freelancer setups, such as:

Remote fitness challenges
Initiate fitness or wellness challenges where team members can participate and update each other on their progress, encouraging healthy competition and camaraderie. This helped individuals to overcome partial loneliness but also helped some individuals start doing exercise.

Virtual talent show
Host a virtual talent show where team members can showcase their hobbies or talents, fostering a sense of community and appreciation for each other's unique abilities. This has been a lot of fun, although it initially took some time and effort to take off.

Online book or film club
Start a book or film club where team members can discuss a chosen book or movie each month, encouraging intellectual

discussion and personal sharing. Something that also allows further learning from each other and creates deeper bonds.

Health and wellness programs
Offer online wellness programs, such as yoga or meditation sessions, which can help reduce feelings of loneliness and improve overall mental health. This has been the most useful way to overcome loneliness. Individuals were looking forward to those sessions.

Virtual escape rooms
Design virtual escape room challenges tailored to the team, encouraging problem-solving and collaboration in an entertaining and engaging virtual setting.

The rapid progression in technology and artificial intelligence is subject to soon offer solutions to mitigate loneliness, particularly in remote work environments. Several of these forthcoming opportunities include:

Virtual Reality (VR) office spaces
Create a VR workspace where workers can interact in a simulated office environment, complete with virtual meeting rooms and coffee areas for informal chats.

Augmented Reality (AR) team building
Utilize AR technology for team-building activities, where remote workers can engage in collaborative tasks or games overlayed onto their physical environment.

AI-Powered personal assistants
Develop personalized AI assistants for each team member, capable of offering conversation, reminders for breaks, and even suggesting networking opportunities with colleagues based on shared interests.

Holographic co-workers
Implement holographic technology with lifelike avatars of team members during meetings or casual catchups, enhancing the sense of presence and connection.

Mindfulness and empathy robots
Use robots or AI tools designed to lead mindfulness exercises or empathy-building activities, helping team members reduce stress and feel more connected.

Digital time capsules
The concept of digital time capsules, where workers can deposit messages, photos, or videos, presents a unique way to build community in a remote setting. These capsules, scheduled to be opened at a predetermined future date, cultivate a sense of excitement and collective anticipation. For gig workers, this becomes an engaging method to reminisce about past projects, colleagues, and the overall work environment. It is a practice that not only bridges the gap of distance but also strengthens bonds by reflecting on shared experiences and anticipating future revelations together.

As leaders, it is easy to overlook the isolation or loneliness that remote workers might experience. To ensure their well-being, it is crucial to regularly gauge their sentiments. This can be achieved through conducting surveys, maintaining consistent check-ins, and establishing robust channels for feedback. These steps are essential in understanding and addressing the unique challenges faced by remote employees.

"Performance should be an expectation of employment and it is the leaders' job to create an environment where maximum performance is possible."
Rob Burn

Performance and Outcome Management

In the sphere of performance and outcome management for remote and gig teams, the focus is on aligning expectations with results, fostering a culture of experimentation, managing the dynamics of team engagement, and celebrating success. This approach is crucial for ensuring that team members not only understand their goals but are also motivated to achieve them innovatively. It involves balancing the drive for results with the need for creative freedom, allowing teams to explore new ideas while maintaining a clear view of desired outcomes. As we proceed, we will dive into the nuances of clarity on expectations and outcomes, embrace the spirit of experimentation, understand the dynamics of the sweet tension concept, and recognize the importance of celebrating success. Each of these subsections provides valuable insights into managing performance and outcomes in a way that is both effective and inspiring for remote and gig workforces.

1. Clarity on expectations and outcomes

In today's rapidly changing work environment, where remote roles, gig jobs, and freelancing are becoming more common, the clarity of expectations between leaders and their teams becomes crucial. As a leader, it is vital to convey not just what is expected from team members but also why these expectations exist. This approach is essential for several reasons.

Clear expectations provide a roadmap for success. In traditional office settings, the proximity to supervisors and frequent in-person interactions naturally creates opportunities for clarifying doubts and expectations. However, in remote or gig work, these interactions are limited or non-existent. Without clear guidance, remote workers might feel adrift, uncertain about priorities, and unclear about how their work aligns with the organization's goals.

Understanding the "why" behind expectations empowers workers. It helps them see the bigger picture and their role in it. This insight is particularly important for remote workers and freelancers who might not have regular exposure to the company's broader strategy. When they understand the purpose behind their tasks, they are more likely to feel engaged and motivated.

Establishing well defined expectations help in building trust. Remote or gig work often rely on a foundation of trust between the leaders and the workers. When expectations are communicated effectively, it demonstrates respect and consideration for the worker's role in the organization. This mutual understanding fosters a positive work environment, even in a virtual space.

Precisely articulated expectations set the stage for accountability. Remote and gig workers, knowing exactly what is expected of them, can take ownership of their tasks and responsibilities. This sense of responsibility leads to higher productivity and a greater sense of achievement.

Well-defined expectations play a key role in overcoming cultural and linguistic differences. Remote and gig work often involves people from various parts of the world, each with their unique work culture and communication style. Clearly stated expectations and outcomes ensure that everyone is on the same page, reducing misunderstandings and conflicts.

Setting clear expectations aids in conflict resolution and performance management. When both parties, the leaders and the workers, are aligned on the expected outcomes, it becomes easier to address issues and discrepancies. This provides a framework within which performance can be evaluated fairly and constructively.

However, articulating expectations is not just a one-way street. It involves an ongoing dialogue where feedback from remote workers and freelancers is equally valued. This exchange ensures that the expectations remain realistic and aligned with the capabilities and resources available to the team.

Setting clear expectations and explaining the reasons behind them is fundamental in remote and gig work environments. It guides, motivates, and aligns the team towards common goals, fostering a productive and positive working relationship. As the nature of work continues to evolve, the ability to communicate expectations effectively will remain a key skill for any successful leader.

Remote, gig-freelance work is a very dynamic world, and in this area, the art of leadership takes on new dimensions. Unlike their local, in-office counterparts, leaders of such dispersed teams face unique challenges in setting expectations and defining outcomes. This environment demands not just a shift in tools and techniques but also a transformation in leadership style, especially when it comes to communicating expectations and desired outcomes.

The first challenge lies in the absence of shared physical space. This lack of face-to-face interaction can lead to misunderstandings or a sense of disconnect. To bridge this gap, a caring leader might adopt a practice of regular, detailed communication. This does not mean just sending out more emails; it is about engaging in meaningful conversations, whether through video calls or chat platforms, where expectations are not just stated but discussed. It is about creating a virtual open-door policy, where team members feel comfortable seeking clarification and leaders can offer guidance in real time.

Another hurdle, as discussed in previous sections of this book, is the diversity of remote and gig teams. These teams are often spread across different time zones and have varied cultural backgrounds. This diversity, while a strength, can make setting uniform expectations challenging. A leader skilled in communication can turn this challenge into an opportunity by personalizing their approach. This means taking the time to understand the individual working styles and cultural contexts of team members and tailoring the communication of expectations accordingly. It is about acknowledging diversity and making it a part of the team's strength.

In remote settings, the tangible markers of progress and success can be less visible. A caring leader can address this by making outcomes and goals highly visible and regularly updated. This could involve using project management tools, not just as a tracking mechanism but as a dynamic storyboard for the team's journey. It is about celebrating milestones, however small, and ensuring that everyone understands how their work contributes to the bigger picture.

Whether hosting our monthly virtual All Hearts meetings (a rebranded version of the traditional All Hands meetings), crafting exciting short videos to highlight and celebrate achievements, or joining spontaneous group calls virtually, all these activities have really worked well in the organizations I led. Overcommunication in a remote or gig-freelancing context is not only necessary but also highly effective. Such proactive and extensive communication is strongly recommended to ensure the success of these work environments. The flexibility that characterizes remote and gig work can also lead to ambiguity in roles and responsibilities. To counter this, effective leaders can implement structured check-ins and goal-setting sessions. These are not just procedural meetings but opportunities for team members to share their progress, set new targets, and realign their efforts with the organization's objectives. It is a practice that brings clarity and direction, fostering a sense of purpose and alignment among team members. What has proven to be effective is conducting check-ins and meetings very frequently, approximately every two to three weeks. In every organization, whether a bustling business or a dedicated non-profit, goals and objectives are the guiding stars. These goals, however, should not just be understood; they need to be embraced, not merely dictated. Reflecting on my experiences across various organizations, I have often seen how the outcomes expected of teams are sometimes just handed down to them, devoid of context or explanation. This approach can leave those tasked with meeting these goals somewhat adrift, unable to fully commit their hearts and efforts to the cause.

For individuals and teams to wholeheartedly strive towards these objectives, they must grasp the whys behind them. Understanding the purpose of these expectations is crucial to understanding what is in it for them, the organization, the customers, shareholders, or beneficiaries. This comprehension is a key motivator, aligning personal and organizational goals in a meaningful way.

It is important to acknowledge that the reasons behind specific expectations might differ from the overarching purpose or mission of the organization or community we lead. While the outcomes generally support the ultimate vision or mission, the rationale behind each key performance indicator (KPI) or expected result needs to be clearly articulated and explained rather than simply told or dictated.

Leadership in this context goes beyond setting objectives. It involves engaging in a dialogue and gathering initial feedback on the feasibility and reception of these outcomes. Constantly taking the pulse of the team is essential to gauge if the outcomes are achievable and to understand what support the team needs to succeed. A leader must recognize that seemingly impossible objectives can become attainable with the right people and tools, provided the "whys" are thoroughly explained.

Furthermore, the role of a leader includes ongoing, effective communication about the organization's progress toward these goals. It is about being open with concerns, recognizing areas for improvement, and continuously listening to feedback. Providing the right tools and resources is not just a responsibility; it is a commitment to the team and the organization's success.

Exploring the impact of clear versus unclear expectations in teams and individual performance reveals crucial insights into workplace dynamics and productivity. According to a Gallup study[26], only about half of workers strongly agree that they understand what is expected of them at work. This uncertainty in expectations poses a significant challenge in achieving performance goals. Managers and leaders play a pivotal role in this regard, as their key responsibilities include setting clear expectations and goals, holding workers accountable, and providing support and feedback. These actions not only clarify what is expected of employees but also significantly contribute to employee engagement. The Gallup analysis emphasizes three core elements for success: achievement, accountability, and accessibility.

Achievement involves establishing clear expectations and goals, which inspires high performance. Accountability entails regular performance feedback and holding workers accountable for meeting expectations. Accessibility means that managers or leaders should be approachable and responsive to employee needs. These factors are closely linked to worker engagement, which in turn influences business outcomes like productivity and profitability.

For instance, the study found that among workers who strongly agree that their manager or leader helps set work priorities, 38% are engaged with their work, compared to only 4% engagement among those who disagree. Similarly, worker engagement is higher when managers or leaders are perceived as holding workers accountable for their performance and being approachable for questions.

The study also highlighted that in Germany, while managers or leaders are generally good at meeting workers' needs for accountability and accessibility, they are less effective in supporting workers' achievement needs. Only about one-third of workers strongly agree that their manager or leader helps them set performance goals, and around 38% strongly agree that their manager or leader supports them in setting work priorities. The implication is clear: when managers or leaders help workers set work priorities and performance goals, they empower them to work autonomously, take the initiative, and be more engaged.

I believe that clear expectations are vital for high performance in teams and individuals. They foster a sense of direction, accountability, and engagement, which are key drivers of productivity and job satisfaction. Managers and leaders play a critical role in this process by setting clear goals, providing regular feedback, and being accessible to support employee needs. Conversely, unclear expectations can lead to disengagement and underperformance, underscoring the importance of clarity in communication and goal setting.

In essence, the journey to achieving organizational goals is a shared one. It requires a leader who not only sets the course but also walks alongside the team, understanding, explaining, and navigating every step of the way. It is about creating an environment where goals are not just assignments but missions understood, shared, and pursued by everyone.

2. Experimentation

The relentless rhythm of repetitive work and an unchanging cadence of tasks have long shaped the perspective of labor across various industries, often casting a shadow on the well-being and productivity of workers. Tracing the impacts of monotonous labor through history offers a revealing insight into its multifaceted consequences.

During the Industrial Revolution, the emergence of factory-based work epitomized the essence of repetitiveness. Workers, including children, were subjected to long hours of monotonous tasks, which not only diminished their physical health due to harsh working conditions but also led to a stifling of creativity and mental exhaustion. The assembly lines of the early 20th century, popularized by Henry Ford's automobile factories, further entrenched this trend. While these lines significantly boosted production efficiency, they also reduced workers to mere cogs in a machine, performing the same task repeatedly, often leading to a sense of alienation and a lack of fulfillment.

In the mid-20th century, the Hawthorne Studies[27], conducted at the Western Electric Hawthorne Works, brought to light the psychological impacts of work environments. The Western Electric Hawthorne Works, during the time of these studies, was primarily engaged in manufacturing telephone equipment. As a major industrial factory, it produced a variety of telecommunications products, including telephone systems and components, which were critical to the expanding telecommunications infrastructure of that era. This manufacturing plant not only played a key role in advancing communication technology but also became a pivotal site for groundbreaking research in industrial and organizational psychology. These studies revealed that workers were not just motivated by pay or working conditions but also by social factors and variety in their work. This was a significant shift in understanding the human element in workspaces, recognizing that monotonous work could negatively impact morale and productivity.

As we progressed into the late 20th and early 21st centuries, the proliferation of technology and the rise of service-oriented jobs brought a new dimension to the issue. Data entry jobs, call centers, and other forms of repetitive office work led to issues like burnout, a term first coined by psychologist Herbert Freudenberger in the

1970s. Burnout encapsulates exhaustion, cynicism, and reduced professional efficacy resulting from prolonged repetitive work.

The physical toll of repetitive work is also well-documented. Repetitive Strain Injury (RSI), a condition characterized by pain or discomfort in muscles, nerves, and tendons due to repetitive motion or overuse, became increasingly recognized towards the end of the 20th century. This condition is often associated with continuous, repetitive tasks and was particularly noted among office workers using computers. RSI exemplifies the physical ramifications of unvarying work patterns, underscoring the need for ergonomic considerations and varied work routines to prevent such injuries. However, the impact of repetitive work is not confined to physical and psychological strains alone. It also encapsulates a broader socio-economic dimension. Historically, jobs characterized by repetitive tasks have been more vulnerable to automation. The Luddite movement of the early 19th century, where English workers destroyed weaving machinery as a form of protest, is a prime example. They feared, rightly, that their skills and labor were becoming obsolete in the face of mechanization.

In today's digital world, despite its constant change, the situation is, in most cases, the same. The same type of work, same customers, same objectives, same tools, and same processes impact the workers, and even more when they are working remotely or as a gig-freelancer.

The history of repetitive work is essentially a story about physical hardship, mental exhaustion, and shifts in society and economy. It underscores the need for a work environment that values variety, creativity, and the human element, paving the way for discussions on innovative leadership models that can transform the future of work, especially in remote, gig, or freelancer organizations. This future vision of leadership would need to embrace experimentation and flexibility, addressing the deep-rooted challenges of repetitive work that history has so vividly illustrated.

My approach in leading fully remote workforces has been one of a relentless pursuit of innovation and experimentation. Irrespective of the efficiency of our tools and processes, we have consistently embraced the challenge of bringing to life a variety of small-scale experiments. This strategy has proven instrumental in fostering collaboration and connection among workers while also enabling leadership to gain deeper insights into their teams. By analyzing data with a curious mindset, asking "What if ?" and initiating experiments, whether brief or extended, we have been able to disrupt the mundane flow of work. This disruption not only alleviates monotony but also yields valuable learnings and innovations, which are then disseminated across the wider organization.

In my professional journey, I have realized that learning is a cornerstone that motivates me and many others. Such experimentation is crucial not just for breaking monotony or feeling productive but, more importantly, for fostering a culture of learning and innovation. This culture not only enriches our professional lives but also propels us forward, individually and collectively, towards greater achievements and understandings.

Experimentation in the context of remote, gig, and freelance work is more than a mere strategy; it is a vital catalyst that rejuvenates the working experience, enhances leadership insights, fosters connections, drives innovation, and highlights the importance of continuous learning.

At the core of the remote work experience often lies a sense of routine and predictability. While this can provide stability, it also risks sliding into monotony. Experimentation serves as an antidote to this. Encouraging remote workers to engage in experimentation, whether through exploring new software, adopting different work methodologies, or altering their schedules, injects a sense of freshness and excitement into their daily tasks. This not only disrupts monotony but also enhances engagement and job satisfaction. A freelancer experimenting with innovative tools, for example, might find more efficient ways to manage tasks, thereby improving their work-life balance and overall well-being.

For leaders who oversee remote teams, experimenting offers insight into the varied abilities and inclinations of their team members. Observing how individuals adapt to new challenges or technologies provides leaders with invaluable insights. Such understanding is crucial in tailoring leadership approaches to suit each team member, ultimately fostering a more harmonious and productive work environment. This could involve experimenting with various communication styles or feedback mechanisms to find the most effective way to connect with and motivate the team.

In terms of building connections among remote workers, experimentation plays a key role. When remote teams collaborate on experiments, such as testing a new project management tool or tackling a creative challenge, it creates a shared experience that can bridge the physical distance. These collaborative efforts help in building a sense of community and teamwork, which is often challenging in a remote setting. Through such shared experiences, workers not only contribute to the project at hand but also develop interpersonal relationships, enhancing team cohesion and morale.

Another significant aspect of experimentation in remote and gig work environments is its role in driving innovation. When workers are encouraged to think outside the box and test new ideas, it leads to a culture of creativity and innovation. This is particularly vital in the gig economy, where staying ahead of the curve can be the difference between success and obsolescence. Experimentation allows workers to not just follow best practices but to create them, keeping the organization at the forefront in its field.

Perhaps most crucially, experimentation nurtures a culture of continuous learning. In the rapidly evolving ecosystem of remote and gig work, adaptability and lifelong learning are key. When workers engage in experimentation, they are not just contributing to immediate projects but are also enhancing their own skill sets and knowledge base. This continuous learning is essential for remote or gig workers, who often do not have the same access to traditional career development opportunities as their counterparts in office settings. Through experimentation, they can continuously evolve and grow professionally, ensuring they remain competitive and relevant in their fields.

From my experience, organizing frequent hackathon events has been a successful strategy. A hackathon is an event where individuals or teams collaborate intensively to innovate or find solutions to pressing or upcoming challenges. It is a creative session, often spanning a few days, where participants brainstorm, develop, and present innovative ideas or technologies. These events offer a refreshing change from everyday tasks, allowing both participants and observers to engage in a learning experience that is also enjoyable and fun. This format not only fosters innovation but also strengthens team bonds and sparks enthusiasm among everyone involved.

3. Celebrating success

Remote and gig-based work is going to become the core of work no later than 2030, and the dynamics of team engagement and motivation will, in this ecosystem, take on new complexities. Central to navigating these challenges is the recognition of the unique contributions of individuals and groups within such environments. In a setting where physical office interactions are absent, and team members often juggle multiple roles or projects, the need for thoughtful recognition becomes not just a nice to have but a crucial ingredient for fostering a sense of belonging and commitment.

At the heart of this paradigm is the understanding that every member of a remote or freelance team brings a distinct set of skills and perspectives. Their contributions, often made in isolation from the rest of the team, can sometimes go unnoticed in the digital workspace. This invisibility can lead to a sense of disconnection, not just from their work but from the organization. It is here that celebration and recognition play a pivotal role. When done with balance and authenticity, it can bridge the gap between isolation and inclusion, transforming the remote work experience into one of engagement and shared purpose.

The positive impacts of well-executed recognition are many. To start with, it acknowledges the individual efforts of team members, validating their work and reinforcing their value within the team. This validation is more than just a feel-good factor; it is a powerful motivator. When people feel seen and appreciated, their engagement and productivity often see a corresponding increase. This is not a mere conjecture. Numerous studies have shown a direct correlation between employee recognition and increased work output. In a remote setting, where traditional forms of motivation might be less effective, recognition can be a potent tool to inspire and energize the workforce.

Recognition helps in cultivating a sense of community and belonging. For remote or gig workers, the sense of being part of a larger whole can sometimes be elusive. Celebrating achievements, whether they be individual milestones or collective successes, fosters a sense of unity and shared identity. It helps build an organizational culture that transcends geographical boundaries, creating a virtual space where every member feels connected and valued. This sense of belonging is crucial not just for the well-being of the employees but for the health of the organization. Teams that share a strong sense of community are more resilient, adaptable, and, ultimately, more successful.

To implement this effectively, it is essential to recognize that one size does not fit all. The nature of recognition should align with the individual or the team's unique context. For some, public accolades may be motivating, while for others, a personal note of thanks might carry more weight. The key is to tailor the recognition to suit the preferences and cultural nuances of each team member, ensuring that it feels genuine and meaningful.

The art of celebrating success is a nuanced yet vital practice, one that is all too easily overlooked in the whirlwind of business operations and competing priorities. This is particularly true in the fast-paced world of remote or gig-freelancing organizations. From my experience, appropriately recognizing and celebrating achievements can serve as a powerful catalyst, propelling an organization forward. My tactical approach in this domain has been twofold, focusing both on individual accomplishments and collective milestones.

Firstly, we place strong emphasis on celebrating the exceptional work delivered by our workforce. Acknowledging these individual contributions is not just a ceremonial act; it is a reaffirmation of each person's value to the organization. Secondly, we also celebrate organizational milestones, recognizing that these successes are the sum of numerous contributions, large and small, from every team member. This dual focus helps create a balanced and inclusive culture of recognition.

The responses we have received, especially from gig workers, have been encouraging. Many shared that in their previous gigs, their efforts went unrecognized, reinforcing a narrative that as "just freelancers," they were somehow less deserving of recognition. I fundamentally challenge this notion. In my view, every team member, whether a full-time employee, contractor, or gig worker, should be entitled to and benefit from acknowledgment for their hard work and achievements.

However, I am mindful not to trivialize recognition through excess. I believe that celebrations that are too frequent could potentially dilute their significance. Hence, I strike a balance, ensuring that each act of recognition is both meaningful and impactful.

Our approach to acknowledging individual or team achievements has been deeply personal and deliberate. Even in managing organizations with over a thousand remote and gig workers, I have made it a priority to connect personally. This involves video calls or personalized videos where I speak directly about the impact of their achievements and how vital their contributions are to the wider organizational goals. The response to these personalized gestures has been overwhelmingly positive, significantly boosting morale and fostering a stronger sense of connection within our remote community.

This practice is not just about celebrating successes; it is about building a culture where every member feels seen, valued, and integral to our collective journey. It shows the importance of a personal touch in an increasingly digital work environment and is a cornerstone in our philosophy of nurturing a thriving, inclusive, and motivated workforce.

4. Sweet tension

The work environment is continuously changing, with remote teams and gig-freelancing not only growing in prevalence but also expected to become even more widespread in the future.

One element of effective leadership in such an environment, which in my experience has proven to be both intriguing and effective, is what I refer to as "sweet tension." This term encapsulates a unique approach to leading teams and motivation, especially crucial in the less structured and often isolated environments of remote or gig work. At its core, sweet tension is about maintaining a deliberate, subtle level of challenge within the team. It is not about inciting conflict or pressure but fostering an atmosphere where complacency is replaced with a consistent, positive state of readiness and engagement. This concept is like an athlete who continues to train rigorously even after achieving a significant milestone; it is about keeping the muscles warm and the reflexes sharp and being ready for the next challenge.

In traditional office settings, the physical presence of peers and leaders naturally creates a certain dynamic tension. However, in remote or gig environments, where physical cues and face-to-face interactions are scarce, instilling and maintaining this sweet tension becomes both a challenge and a necessity. As we delve deeper into this concept, we will explore why sweet tension is particularly vital in remote teams, how it benefits such teams, and how leaders can effectively implement and sustain it.

This section argues that the strategic application of sweet tension is not just beneficial but essential for the success and longevity of remote or gig-freelancing teams. By maintaining this delicate balance, leaders can cultivate environments where innovation, vigilance, and collaboration thrive, ensuring their teams are not just functioning but excelling in the ever-changing ecosystem of the modern workplace.

The conceptual framework for understanding sweet tension begins with its definition. At its essence, sweet tension is a strategic management approach that fosters a continuous, positive state of challenge within a team. Unlike conventional stress, which can be detrimental, sweet tension is about keeping a team on its toes - alert, focused, and ready for innovation. It is a delicate balance between comfort and challenge, ensuring team members are neither complacent nor overwhelmed. This concept draws from psychological principles like the Yerkes-Dodson law, which suggests that there is an optimal level of arousal for peak performance. Too little stress leads to underperformance due to complacency, while too much can cause anxiety and burnout. Sweet tension, therefore, aims to find that sweet spot where team members are sufficiently stimulated to achieve their best work without crossing into negative stress territory.

From a motivational perspective, sweet tension aligns with the concepts of intrinsic motivation and flow. It creates an environment where team members are engaged in their work not just for external rewards but for the satisfaction and challenge it brings. This approach fosters a state of flow, where individuals are fully immersed and energized by their activities, experiencing a sense of fulfillment and productivity. In organizational behavior, sweet tension resonates with the idea of transformational leadership, where leaders inspire and motivate their teams to exceed expectations. By maintaining this tension, leaders encourage continuous growth and learning, pushing their teams toward innovation and excellence while ensuring they feel supported and valued.

Implementing sweet tension requires a nuanced understanding of each team member's capabilities and stress thresholds. It is about assigning challenging but achievable goals, providing timely feedback, and creating an environment where risks and creativity are encouraged and failures are viewed as learning opportunities.

The conceptual framework of sweet tension is rooted in the understanding that the right amount of challenge and engagement can propel a team to new heights. It leverages psychological and motivational theories to create an environment where team members are continuously engaged, motivated, and prepared to tackle challenges innovatively and effectively.

The necessity of sweet tension in team management, particularly in remote or gig-freelancing environments, is grounded in several compelling arguments. Firstly, in the absence of traditional workplace structures and the physical presence of leaders and peers, remote teams may be prone to a sense of isolation and disconnection. Sweet tension acts as a catalyst, fostering a sense of collective purpose and engagement, which is crucial for maintaining productivity and team cohesion.

Sweet tension encourages a culture of continuous improvement and adaptability. In today's rapidly changing business landscape, resting on one's laurels can lead to obsolescence. By maintaining a level of positive challenge, teams are constantly motivated to seek better solutions, innovate, and stay ahead of the curve. This is especially vital in gig and remote settings where team members may be working on diverse projects with varying degrees of complexity and innovation requirements. Moreover, this concept aligns with the intrinsic nature of human motivation. People are generally driven by challenges that stretch their capabilities but are still within their reach. Sweet tension provides this balance, offering tasks that are neither too easy to induce boredom nor too difficult to cause frustration. In remote settings, where direct supervision and immediate feedback are limited, such an approach can significantly boost self-motivation and accountability.

Another argument in favor of sweet tension is its role in preparing teams for unforeseen challenges. In remote and gig environments, where team members may be spread across different time zones and locations, the ability to swiftly adapt to change and navigate uncertainties is paramount. Sweet tension keeps teams in a state of readiness, ensuring they are not caught off-guard by sudden shifts in project dynamics or market trends.

Sweet tension also plays a significant role in enhancing team dynamics and collaboration. When a team collectively faces challenges, they learn to work more cohesively, share knowledge, and support each other. In remote teams, where physical distance can create barriers to collaboration, sweet tension can serve as a unifying force, bringing team members together in pursuit of common goals.

It is important to address the unique application of sweet tension in the context of gig workers and freelancers. These individuals often work on short-term projects and may feel disconnected from the broader goals of the organization. Implementing sweet tension in these scenarios involves creating a sense of belonging and aligning individual tasks with overarching organizational objectives. It ensures that even short-term contributors are fully engaged and contributing to the team's success.

However, the implementation of sweet tension must be carefully managed to avoid potential pitfalls. One significant risk is the misinterpretation of this concept as a justification for overloading employees with work or setting unrealistic goals. It is crucial to distinguish sweet tension from harmful stress. Sweet tension is about creating an environment where challenges are seen as opportunities for growth, not as threats or burdens.

When the idea of sweet tension is skillfully implemented, it can bring about a multitude of advantages for remote and gig-freelancing teams. Now, let's dive a bit deeper into these benefits:

Enhanced team performance and productivity
Sweet tension creates an environment where team members are continuously motivated to push their boundaries. This leads to improved performance as individuals and teams strive to meet the challenges set before them. In remote settings, where self-motivation is key, sweet tension helps maintain an elevated level of productivity as team members are engaged in meaningful and challenging work.

Increased innovation and creativity
One of the primary advantages of maintaining sweet tension is the cultivation of an innovative mindset. When team members are encouraged to think beyond the status quo and are challenged to find innovative solutions, creativity thrives. This is particularly beneficial in gig and remote work, where diverse perspectives and skills can lead to groundbreaking ideas and solutions.

Improved adaptability and flexibility
Teams accustomed to sweet tension are more adaptable to change. This flexibility is crucial in today's fast-paced business environment, where market trends and technologies are constantly evolving. Remote or gig teams, often working in dynamic and unpredictable settings, benefit greatly from being conditioned to expect and respond effectively to change.

Enhanced team cohesion and collaboration
Sweet tension can also foster a stronger sense of unity and collaboration within the team. When members collectively face challenges and work towards common goals, it strengthens team bonds. For remote teams, where physical distance can be a barrier, this sense of cohesion is invaluable for maintaining a collaborative and supportive team culture.

Development of skills and competencies
Continuous challenge leads to continuous learning. Team members in an environment of sweet tension are constantly developing new skills and honing existing ones. This continuous personal and professional development is particularly advantageous in gig and freelance settings, where individuals must frequently adapt to different roles and projects.

Preparation for future challenges
Teams nurtured in an environment of sweet tension are better prepared for future challenges. This proactive approach to team management ensures that teams do not become complacent but are always ready and equipped to tackle new and unforeseen challenges, which is a vital trait in the ever-changing landscape of remote work.

Increased employee satisfaction and retention
Finally, sweet tension can lead to higher levels of job satisfaction. When team members are engaged, challenged, and see the value in their work, their overall job satisfaction increases. This is especially significant in remote or gig environments, where physical detachment from the workspace can impact one's connection to the job. Higher satisfaction levels subsequently lead to better worker retention rates.

As you can see, the benefits of sweet tension are many, impacting not just the immediate productivity and performance of the team but also fostering a culture of innovation, adaptability, and continuous growth. These benefits are particularly pertinent to remote and gig-freelancing teams, where the traditional levels of motivation and engagement are often absent or diminished.

Let us now dive into practical applications of sweet tension in various work environments, particularly focusing on remote and gig-freelancing teams, to understand how this concept plays out in real-world scenarios:

Scenario 1
Consider a tech start-up in a rapid growth phase, with team members dispersed across continents. The leadership, recognizing the challenges of keeping a remote team engaged and innovative, decides to introduce hackathons and innovation challenges. These initiatives are not just about fostering creativity; they are strategically designed to maintain a level of sweet tension within the team. As team members engage in these challenges, they find themselves pushed out of their comfort zones, collaborating intensively despite physical distances. The outcomes are remarkable; the team not only develops groundbreaking products but also forms a robust culture of continuous learning and adaptation, proof of the effectiveness of sweet tension in maintaining high performance and innovation in a remote setting.

Scenario 2
A global consulting firm employs a mix of permanent staff and gig workers, often assembling teams for specific projects. Here, sweet tension is manifested through a unique approach to project management. The firm introduces innovation sprints within each project lifecycle, where team members are encouraged to question existing methodologies and propose innovative solutions to complex problems. These sprints create a dynamic work environment where even temporary team members feel deeply involved and motivated. The result is a significant increase in both the quality of work and client satisfaction. In this context, sweet tension serves as a bridge, connecting diverse team members and fostering a sense of unity and purpose, which is crucial in a setting where teams are frequently reformed and restructured.

Scenario 3

A multinational corporation transitioning to remote work. To combat potential disengagement and loss of team synergy, the company leadership implements a series of cross-functional virtual workshops. These workshops are designed to encourage employees from different departments to collaborate on companywide challenges, ranging from sustainability initiatives to process optimization. The introduction of these workshops creates sweet tension, as employees are encouraged to step outside their usual roles and collaborate with colleagues from different areas of the business. This strategy not only leads to innovative solutions to company challenges but also enhances inter-departmental understanding and cooperation.

In this remote work context, sweet tension successfully mitigates the risk of the forming of isolated groups, keeping the team cohesive and aligned with the company's broader goals. In each of these scenarios, sweet tension acts as a catalyst for growth, innovation, and cohesion. Whether in a fast-paced start-up, a project-based consulting firm, or a large corporation adapting to remote work, maintaining a delicate balance of challenge and engagement leads to positive outcomes. These examples demonstrate that when applied thoughtfully, sweet tension can be a powerful tool for leaders managing remote or gig-freelancing teams, helping to drive performance, foster innovation, and ensure a strong, collaborative team culture.

Creating a sweet tension environment, particularly in remote or gig-freelancer settings, is challenging, yet my many years of experience have shown its effectiveness. Implementing this concept requires subtlety; it is not something you openly declare as a sweet tension exercise. Instead, it is a discreet approach, often not even shared with the immediate leadership team. The key is to subtly foster this environment, enhancing productivity and engagement without explicitly stating its purpose, thus maintaining a natural and organic work atmosphere that encourages innovation and progress in these unique work settings.

It was several years ago that, in a burst of inspiration and innovation, I stumbled upon what I would come to call the "sweet tension" concept. At that time, I was utterly convinced of its universal applicability, a one-size-fits-all solution to stimulate any team in any circumstance. However, the path of discovery is often paved with missteps, and mine was no different. I vividly recall instances where I enthusiastically introduced sweet tension to teams already brewing under the weight of their duties and daily stress. The atmosphere was already charged, and my well-intentioned addition only served to tip the scales toward overload.

The consequences were immediate and eye-opening. The team dynamics began to deteriorate. I watched as, despite my best intentions, a few remarkable talents slipped through my fingers, unable to thrive under the unnecessary strain I had inadvertently introduced. These were enlightening moments, stark reminders that even the most promising strategies can falter if not applied with careful consideration.

It was a learning journey steeped in humility and self-reflection. Each misstep was a lesson, each loss a stark reminder of the delicate balance required in leadership. Through these experiences, I refined my understanding of sweet tension, learning to gauge the pulse of a team, to sense when to introduce a challenge, and when to hold back. These lessons were hard-earned but invaluable. They taught me that the art of leadership is as much about timing and perception as it is about vision and strategy.

Individual variability in stress thresholds further complicates the application of sweet tension. The diversity in a team means that a level of challenge that energizes one member might be paralyzing for another. This calls for a nuanced understanding of each team member's capacity for stress and challenge. In remote work settings, it becomes even more challenging for leaders to discern the subtle signs of distress or disengagement among team members. The lack of real-time, face-to-face interactions necessitates a more attentive and empathetic leadership approach. Cultural and personal value systems significantly influence how individuals respond to challenges. What might be motivating in one cultural context could be perceived as overly demanding in another. This highlights the importance of cultural sensitivity and adaptability in leadership. Additionally, sweet tension heavily leans on intrinsic motivation, which can vary widely among individuals. Not everyone is equally self-motivated, and some might require more external stimuli to stay engaged and productive.

To successfully implement sweet tension and mitigate its downsides, leaders must adopt a tailored approach, recognizing the unique needs, thresholds, and circumstances of each team member. This personalized strategy ensures that challenges are motivating rather than overwhelming. Establishing a culture of open communication is crucial. It encourages team members to voice their concerns and provides leaders with essential feedback to adjust the level of challenge appropriately.

Setting realistic and achievable goals is another key aspect. These goals should stretch the team's abilities without pushing them into a zone of excessive stress. Supporting the team, where leaders recognize efforts, celebrate successes, and provide resources for overcoming challenges, is equally vital. This nurturing environment helps maintain high morale and motivation. Continuous monitoring and adjustment of the sweet tension level is essential. Leaders should use feedback and performance metrics to gauge the effectiveness of their strategies, making adjustments as necessary. This agile approach ensures that the team remains on the right track, motivated, and productive.

I encourage you to approach these principles with thoughtfulness and a keen awareness of your team's current state. Remember, sweet tension is a powerful tool, but its success depends on the nuanced understanding of when and how it should be utilized.

"Leadership in the digital age is not about managing from the top; it is about fostering a sense of belonging and purpose within a remote workforce."
David Wilson

Building and Sustaining Community

Building and sustaining a community in the context of remote and gig workforces is a journey of nurturing connections and shared values. It is about creating a space where individuals, regardless of their physical locations, feel a sense of belonging and purpose. This involves not just connecting people with each other but fostering a culture where community and social good are at the forefront. Such an environment encourages collaboration, support, and a shared commitment to common goals. It is a process that requires continuous effort and dedication to maintain the social fabric of an organization. As we introduce the subsections, we will discover the intricacies of catalyzing prosperity and community, the art of community building, and the importance of social good activities in crafting a cohesive and thriving remote team community.

1. Connecting people with each other

A fascinating yet often overlooked aspect of a caring leader is the power of connection. The most impactful leaders and successful individuals do not just excel in their personal capabilities; they also act as catalysts, connecting people with one another. This unique role goes beyond traditional notions of leadership or entrepreneurship. It is about understanding the profound impact that fostering relationships and networks can have, not just on the individuals involved but on the broader community and even the world at large.

Imagine a scenario where a successful business leader introduces two emerging entrepreneurs, sparking a collaboration that leads to a groundbreaking innovation. Or consider a community lead who brings together diverse groups, leading to a stronger, more cohesive neighborhood. These scenarios illustrate the essence of being a catalyst; it is not about being at the forefront but about being the bridge that connects people, ideas, and resources.

This role of a connector is subtle yet powerful. Successful people who excel in this area often have a keen sense of observation. They understand not only the strengths and needs of the people around them but also the synergies that can arise from bringing the right individuals together. It is about seeing the potential in a connection before it has even been made.

Acting as a connector is deeply rooted in the concept of community and prosperity. The prosperity generated from these connections is not just financial; it is also about the exchange of ideas, support, and inspiration. When people are connected, they share resources, knowledge, and opportunities, creating a ripple effect that extends far beyond the initial interaction.

This aspect of connection is especially crucial in today's interconnected world. With the arrival of global communication networks and social media, the potential for impactful connections has increased. Successful individuals who harness this power are not just building networks; they are working to build a more collaborative and innovative society.

But why do these connectors do what they do? Is it purely for personal gain, or is there something more? Often, the motivation lies in a genuine desire to see others succeed and grow. These individuals derive satisfaction not from personal accolades but from witnessing the growth and success that their connections enable.

The impact of these connections can be far-reaching. They can spark new business ventures, social movements, artistic collaborations, and more. The benefits are not only economic but also social and cultural, contributing to a more vibrant and resilient community.

The role of successful people and leaders as catalysts in connecting others is proof of the power of human relationships. It is a reminder that success is not just about individual achievement but about how we use our position, knowledge, and networks to uplift others. As we move forward in an increasingly connected world, the value of these human connectors will only grow, making them not just successful individuals but architects of a more collaborative and prosperous future.

The role of a catalyst leader in fostering connections is a nuanced and vital aspect of modern leadership, and its intricacies and impacts are profound. These leaders are not just the heads of organizations or groups; they are the architects of networks and the creators of relationships. Their ability to bring people together transcends professional interactions, creating synergies that foster community, innovation, and prosperity.

At the heart of the catalyst leader's approach is the understanding that the success of an organization or community is deeply intertwined with the richness of connections among its members. They recognize that when individuals with diverse skills, backgrounds, and aspirations are brought together, the potential for innovation, problem-solving, and growth is immense.

This process begins with an insightful yet non-intrusive gathering of information. During onboarding or through regular interactions, catalyst leaders collect voluntary information from individuals, such as hobbies, spoken languages, career aspirations, learning interests, personal skills, or travel dreams. This information, gathered respectfully and ethically, forms the foundation upon which meaningful connections are built.

The next step involves identifying potential connections through this information, sometimes with the aid of artificial intelligence tools. For example, a leader might connect someone wishing to learn a new language with a native speaker within the organization. Similarly, linking individuals with similar travel dreams can lead to enriching conversations and shared experiences that benefit both their professional and personal lives.

However, the essence of a catalyst leader's role extends beyond data and into the domain of deep conversations and keen observations. Through regular, meaningful interactions, these leaders gain insights into the aspirations, strengths, and potential of their team members. This understanding allows them to facilitate connections that are not just based on shared interests but also on complementary skills and potential synergies.

Catalyst leaders also understand the importance of timing and context in making these connections. They recognize that the right introduction at the right moment can be the key to unlocking a fruitful collaboration or a lasting relationship. They are skilled at creating an environment where such connections can flourish, be it through formal networking events, casual social gatherings, or even digital communication platforms. These leaders extend their connection-facilitating role beyond the confines of their organization. They strive to connect their team members with individuals and opportunities in the broader industry or community. This approach not only enriches the lives of the individuals involved but also enhances the organization's network and reputation.

Another critical aspect of being a catalyst leader is the facilitation of the connection process. They do not just introduce people to each other; they also help in setting up the context and purpose of the connection. This might involve explaining the commonalities or potential areas of collaboration to both parties, thus easing the initial interaction and setting the stage for a fruitful relationship.

The impact of such leadership is far-reaching. It leads to a more engaged and satisfied workforce, as individuals feel valued and seen for more than just their professional skills. It fosters a culture of collaboration and innovation as people with diverse perspectives and skills come together. On a larger scale, it contributes to building a more interconnected and resilient community or industry.

The role of a catalyst leader is crucial in today's interconnected world and is key for remote teams. Their ability to connect people with others not only enhances individual careers and personal lives but also drives organizational growth and societal progress. By understanding the art of connection and practicing it with empathy, insight, and strategic thinking, these leaders are not just managing teams; they are building vibrant, dynamic, and prosperous communities.

The table in the next page can give you a real-life example of how one could leverage information to create connections. The approach applied in the table, is an example for technical support consultants who speak different languages, know Microsoft, Google, and Amazon technologies, and are spread across different countries on the planet.

Information Gathered	Connection Opportunity	Benefit
Language: Speaks Spanish	Connect Spanish-speaking consultants for collaboration on projects.	Leverages language skills in a diverse team.
Career Aspiration: Project Management	Pair less experienced consultants with seasoned project managers.	Aids in career development within the technical domain.
Technical Skill: Google Cloud	Create a knowledge-sharing group with others interested in Google Cloud.	Encourages cross-technology expertise.
Work Pattern: 24x7	Establish a global round-the-clock problem-solving forum.	Utilizes 24x7 work fashion for efficient problem solving.
Soft Skills: Strong Communication	Lead virtual training sessions for those looking to improve soft skills.	Improves soft skills among technically focused team members.
Travel Interest: Different Locations	Organize virtual meet-ups to share travel experiences and tips.	Connects globally located team members.
Experience with Partners	Form a best practices group for those working or aspiring to work with partners.	Leverages experience for collective learning.
Interest in Learning Amazon Cloud Technologies	Pair with colleagues who have expertise in Amazon Cloud.	Promotes cross-training in cloud technologies.
Work Experience: Varied	Host a virtual panel discussion with experienced consultants.	Utilizes the depth of experience in the team.
Technical Skill: Lack of Soft Skills	Pair with colleagues known for excellent soft skills in collaborative projects.	Addresses skill gaps in a practical, engaging manner.

2. Social good activities

In every corner of our world, there are stories that resonate deeply with the heart of a caring leader. Imagine, for a moment, the daily struggle of those who wake up not knowing where their next meal will come from. This hunger is more than just an empty stomach; it is a reminder of the complex challenges our world faces. Hunger is not just a problem in faraway places; it also exists in the hidden parts of busy cities, where families find it hard to get by.

Water, so essential to life, is a scarce commodity for many. In places where the wells run dry, the struggle for clean water is a daily reality. It is not just about droughts; it is about how we share and care for our planet's precious resources. This challenge extends to the pollution of rivers and oceans, where the lifeblood of our planet is tainted, affecting not just the human population but all forms of life.

Education, a key to a better future, remains out of reach for too many children. Born into poverty, they watch the doors of opportunity close before they even have the chance to knock. This lack of access to education is a stark reminder of the deep inequalities that exist in our world. Education is more than just learning to read and write; it is the gateway to understanding, opportunity, and empowerment.

Our planet is showing signs of strain under the weight of pollution and environmental damage. Air pollution and deforestation do not just affect us today; they threaten the future of the next generations. Climate change is no longer a distant threat; it is a present-day crisis that impacts the lives of millions, from rising sea levels threatening coastal communities to extreme weather events wreaking havoc across the globe.

Inequality and the unfair distribution of wealth create a society where the gap between rich and poor seems to only grow wider. This disparity extends to healthcare, access to technology, and basic human rights, painting a picture of a divided world.

In the hustle and bustle of city life, it is easy to overlook those who have no place to call home. Homelessness is more than not having a roof over your head; it is about the many ways our society fails to support its most vulnerable members. It is about the lack of mental health support, the challenges of addiction, and the barriers to re-entering the workforce.

And let's not forget those living in rural areas, often out of sight and out of mind. Their struggles and needs may be less visible, but they are just as real. These communities face unique challenges, from limited access to healthcare and education to the struggles of maintaining traditional ways of life in a rapidly changing world.

As leaders in a world that is increasingly interconnected yet fraught with these challenges, there is a compelling need to act with compassion and vision. Our actions, big or small, can start a ripple of change that reaches far beyond our immediate surroundings. This is the heart of leading a socially conscious organization, whether it is remote, gig-based, or freelance. It is about understanding these issues deeply and committing to being part of the solution, bringing hope and tangible change to those who need it most. In doing so, we do not just address the immediate needs; we build a foundation for a more equitable and sustainable future.

As a leader who has navigated various landscapes, be it remote, local, gig-based, or freelance, I have come to recognize the profound impact of applying the core leadership principles discussed in this book. My most remarkable experiences in leading organizations, where I have gained a lot and built solid relationships with people and communities, have arisen from participating in activities for social good to help those in need. These experiences have taught me the power of transforming unknown remote or gig teams into cohesive units, bound not by proximity but by shared purpose and experiences. How you might ask, can your leadership bridge the vast distances of remote teams or the impersonal nature of gig work? The answer lies in engaging these teams in socially impactful projects.

In today's world, where our awareness of global needs is amplified by technological advances, the call to action is louder than ever. People and institutions around us are in need, and there are issues that cry out for attention and healing. It is here, in the social good initiatives, that I discovered the key to consolidating the culture within my organizations while fostering deep, personal connections among team members.

Establishing funds for social good projects in local or regional areas, started and managed by our organization's members and motivated by the leaders, has proven to be a highly effective and successful strategy. This approach goes beyond traditional team building or corporate social responsibility. It is about creating a shared journey, a collective story where every member, regardless of their location or role, feels personally invested and connected to the cause and, by extension, to each other.

Such initiatives have a twofold impact. First, they bring about tangible positive changes in the communities we aim to serve. We are not just working together; we are working towards something bigger than ourselves, something that makes a real difference in the world. Second, they foster a sense of unity and purpose within the team. As we collaborate on these projects, barriers break down.

Distance becomes irrelevant, and the traditional employer-worker relationship transforms into one of partnership and mutual respect.

Moreover, these social good projects become a part of our personal and professional identities. Team members feel a sense of pride and belonging, knowing they are part of an organization that doesn't just aim for profit but also for a positive impact on society. This shared identity builds trust and empathy, crucial elements for any successful team, especially in remote or gig environments where physical presence is limited.

During the COVID-19 pandemic, the gig-freelancer teams I interacted with came together to develop an initiative they named "Charity Box." This concept involved voluntary weekly donations from individuals. The funds raised were channeled into meaningful causes, such as providing oxygen devices to India during a particularly devastating phase of the pandemic, assisting fellow workers in affording critical surgeries, and aiding in the repair of damages caused by regular typhoons in the Philippines. Remarkably, the Charity Box initiative successfully raised around 35,000 US$ annually. Considering our remote structure, predominantly composed of gig workers, this achievement was particularly remarkable, and such initiatives became part of the DNA of the community.

In my leadership journey, embracing social good has not only expanded the impact of my organizations beyond their immediate goals but also fostered a culture where every member feels connected and valued. This approach has turned unknown teams into families, bridging miles and differences with heart-to-heart connections. When we lead with empathy and a vision for social good, the bonds we create are not just for the moment but for a lifetime.

3. Community building

Across the globe, there exists a vast number and types of communities, both in the digital world and beyond. These communities, often born from intense enthusiasm and passion, represent a diverse spectrum of interests and purposes. While there are a notable number of success stories, it is a common occurrence for many of these communities to fade away or cease operations. The heart of a community lies in the reciprocal exchange among its members, where individuals both contribute to and benefit from the collective.

Typically, communities are guided by one or a few leaders. The sustainability of these communities frequently hinges on the continued involvement and direction provided by these leaders. In the absence of this sustained leadership, many communities tend to dissipate. Additionally, it is not uncommon to observe that the founders of these communities might have underlying motives. Such motives can range from steering the community towards a specific ideology or objective to leveraging the community for financial gains, like attracting advertisers by showcasing the community's activities and engagement.

This phenomenon raises a fundamental question: How can a community be organically formed, nurtured, and evolved over time? It is important to acknowledge that it is perfectly natural for a community to have a life cycle. A community may emerge, flourish for a period, and then dissolve once its founding purpose is achieved, making way for new communities to arise. This cycle of creation, evolution, and dissolution is a dynamic and organic process, reflecting the ever-changing nature of human interests and societal needs.

I want to dive a bit into the different types of communities based on the purpose of their creation, so that a caring leader of a remote or gig-freelancing organization can leverage the concept and move toward the creation or encouragement of the creation of those specific communities. Each of these communities has their pros and cons when it comes to their setup, maintenance, and outcomes.

Communities around the world are diverse, each serving unique purposes based on the interests, needs, and circumstances of their members. In his article on the HelpfulProfessor.com website[28],

Chris Drew discusses various types of communities categorized mainly by their purpose:

Communities of place

These include national, urban, suburban, rural, and neighborhood communities. Each has distinct structures, needs, and focuses; for example, densely populated urban communities rely on peripheral communities for resources, and rural communities often revolve around agrarian lifestyles.

Interest-based communities

These are formed by individuals sharing common interests or passions, like subcultures and countercultures, which align around specific beliefs or interests distinct from the dominant culture. Examples include communities centered around hobbies, sports, love for specific technology or tools, or particular lifestyles.

Identity-based communities

These encompass religious groups, ethnic groups, and communities formed around shared personal characteristics or experiences, like persons with disabilities, hearing-impaired, and elderly communities. These communities often provide support networks and facilitate shared cultural or religious practices.

Professional and business-oriented communities

These include professional communities, guilds, associations, and business or economic communities. They can be based on shared professional interests, hobbies, business advocacy, or economic collaboration at a larger scale, like trade blocks.

Communities for specific purposes

This category includes communities for marketing or brand promotion, educational and informational purposes, entertainment, and activism. They serve specific goals like promoting a brand, disseminating information or education, providing entertainment, or fostering social change.

Action-oriented communities
These communities are focused on enacting change and can include activist groups or organizations working towards specific societal or environmental goals.

Communities of circumstance
Formed due to external situations, these communities bring together people who find themselves in similar life situations, such as migrants or expatriates.

Communities of practice
These are groups of people engaging in the same profession or activities, often focusing on shared professional development and ongoing learning.

Each type of community, whether based on location, interest, identity, profession, or a specific purpose, plays a vital role in fostering social interaction, support, and a sense of belonging among its members, and that, as we have been discussing throughout this book, is one of the core elements to be able to successfully lead a community, especially remote or made up of gig-freelancers.

An effective leader plays a crucial role in fostering community within an organization, either by directly initiating or encouraging the development of such communities. From my professional experience, I have found that forming these communities can be quite straightforward, particularly with the aid of non-personal information collected during the employee onboarding process, provided with the individual's consent. This process involves simply presenting the various available community options that align with the new employees' interests, enabling them to easily locate and engage with these groups from the outset. Therefore, it is vital to clearly define each community, establish a welcoming procedure for new members, and involve dedicated volunteers to actively manage and steer the community. Such well-orchestrated communities are instrumental in connecting people, fostering innovation, facilitating mutual learning, and bringing important issues to the attention of leadership for effective resolution and positive outcomes.

It is equally essential for the organization's leader to actively engage with these communities on a regular basis. This involvement helps them stay attuned to the communities' activities, gauge their overall sentiment, and respond to their needs effectively.

In reflecting on my professional journey, I have realized that the crucial factor for successful communities is choosing the right leaders. For many years, our efforts fell short because we could not find the right people to guide these communities, leading to their eventual decline and failure to achieve their intended purpose. However, through these experiences, we gradually improved our selection process. We have had successes in some areas, meeting our objectives, but the biggest lesson learned is that while forming a community is relatively straightforward, the true challenge lies in keeping it vibrant and active.

From my personal experience related to the challenges of establishing communities, I have understood that the key to a community's survival and success, particularly in a gig and freelancing context with geographically dispersed members, lies in finding and choosing individuals who are deeply passionate and tirelessly dedicated to leading these communities. The following strategies have proven beneficial during the selection process:

Look for demonstrated passion
During interviews or interactions, the candidates could be asked about their previous involvement in communities or group projects. Their level of enthusiasm, commitment, and the impact of their involvement can be indicators of their passion.

To determine a candidate's passion for community leadership, particularly in assessing their previous involvement and the impact they have made, the following three questions could be asked during an interview:

- Can you describe a community project or initiative you have led or been actively involved in?
    - This question helps gauge their direct experience in community engagement and leadership. Pay attention to how they describe their role, the challenges they faced, and the outcomes they achieved.
- What motivated you to get involved in that community, and what were your key contributions?
    - This question aims to uncover their personal drive and commitment. It helps in understanding what aspects of community involvement excite them and how they view their role in fostering community growth.

Assess communication skills
Effective community leaders are excellent communicators. A candidate's ability to articulate ideas, listen actively, and engage in meaningful conversations could be evaluated.

Observe initiative and proactiveness
Candidates who naturally take the initiative and are proactive in their approach are more likely to be effective community drivers. Examples of where the candidate has taken the lead in past projects or situations could be explored.

Evaluate their ability to connect and network

Strong networking skills are crucial for building and nurturing community relationships. Candidate's ability to connect with others, build rapport, and maintain relationships can be assessed.

To evaluate a candidate's networking and relationship-building skills, essential for leading a community, the following interview questions could be asked:

- Can you share an example of how you have built or expanded a professional network or community?
  - This question aims to understand their approach to networking. Look for how they initiate connections, maintain relationships, and leverage these networks for the community's benefit.
- Describe a time when you successfully brought together diverse groups or individuals to achieve a common goal. What was your approach?
  - This question is insightful for assessing their ability to engage with diverse members, understand different perspectives, and unify them towards a shared objective.
- How do you maintain long-term professional relationships, especially in a remote or virtual setting?
  - Given the challenges of managing dispersed communities, this question seeks to gauge their strategies for sustaining relationships over time and distance, which is crucial in a gig and freelancing environment.

Check for alignment with community goals

Candidates' personal or professional goals alignment with the community's objectives could be explored. This alignment increases the likelihood of sustained interest and commitment.

Seek references or testimonials
If possible, seek feedback from previous employers, colleagues, or community members they have worked with. This can provide insights into their ability to inspire and lead a community. A candidate's professional social media profiles can be checked, for example, on LinkedIn, to see if candidates have been involved in community activities or whether their connections have referenced the candidate related to community activities.

Consider adaptability and cultural fit
Community leaders should be adaptable to different environments and fit well with the organizational culture. Their ability to work with diverse groups and adapt to various situations is important.

Test with hypothetical scenarios
Hypothetical scenarios related to community management could be presented to the candidates, and their problem-solving and decision-making skills could be observed.

To evaluate a candidate's problem-solving and decision-making abilities in the context of community management, the following interview questions could be asked to the candidate:

- Describe a complex problem you faced while managing a community. How did you approach the issue, and what was the outcome?
    - This question helps to understand their analytical and problem-solving skills in real-world situations. It provides insight into how they dissect complex issues, strategize solutions, and implement them within a community.
- Can you give an example of a difficult decision you had to make in a community leadership role? How did you arrive at your decision, and what were the consequences?

o This question is intended to assess their decision-making process and ability to handle the repercussions of their choices. It reveals their judgment and accountability in high-stakes situations.

- Imagine you are leading a community that is facing engagement challenges. What steps would you take to identify the causes and revive member participation?
  o This hypothetical scenario evaluates their proactive thinking and strategic planning skills. It shows how they would tackle common community issues, like engagement and participation, and their ability to formulate and execute a revival plan.

Assess long-term commitment

In the gig economy, long-term commitment can be rare. Candidates' views on long-term involvement and assessing their willingness to commit to the community for an extended period could be discussed with them.

Look for empathy and emotional intelligence

Empathy and emotional intelligence are key traits of successful community leaders, as they help in understanding and addressing the needs of community members effectively. Emotional intelligence (EI) is an essential aspect of our personal and professional lives. It is the ability to understand and manage your own emotions while empathizing with others. High emotional intelligence can lead to better relationships, improved decision-making, and greater success in various areas of life.

A range of online tests are available to help you assess and potentially improve your emotional intelligence. Here are some notable ones:

- **Emotional intelligence test by Psychology Today**[29]:
  - o This test offers a free snapshot report and a summary evaluation, with an option to purchase a more detailed analysis.

- **Emotional intelligence test by Psych Tests**[30]:
  - o A comprehensive test that analyzes results and suggests ways to increase overall EI.

- **Alpha High IQ Society's Emotional Intelligence Test**[31]:
  - o This test measures self-awareness and provides insights into practical communication skills and emotional expressions·

Now let's discover the differences between communities created intentionally by a leader versus communities that flourish organically in a remote setup and discuss the pros and cons of each of them:

Especially in remote environments, two predominant types of communities emerge: leader-created and organically formed communities. Leader-created communities are like structured ecosystems, where deliberate planning, clear objectives, and resource allocation are fundamental. These communities mirror the strategic visions of their founders or leaders, much like a botanical garden where each element is purposefully placed and tended. Leader-driven communities, established and guided by organizational leaders or designated managers, are characterized by their structured approach. These communities are often goal-oriented, aligned with organizational objectives, and equipped with resources and clear guidelines. This structure ensures that community activities are purposeful and measurable, offering a clear path toward achieving specific outcomes.

Conversely, organically formed communities resemble natural ecosystems, evolving spontaneously based on shared interests and mutual needs of their members. These communities often emerge in remote work environments, where individuals, despite geographical dispersion, congregate in digital spaces over commonalities. Their growth and sustainability, unpredictable yet vibrant, are like a wildflower meadow, thriving without meticulous planning. My experience suggests that these communities are long-lasting ones and need less maintenance, and therefore, a leader should encourage those communities. Organic communities spring from the common interests or challenges shared among members. These communities are less about fulfilling predefined goals and more about fostering natural, member-driven interactions. They thrive on spontaneity, genuine engagement, and collective member interests, adapting and evolving based on member feedback and participation. The strength of these communities lies in their flexibility and ability to inspire innovation and elevated levels of engagement among members.

The dynamics within these communities offer insightful contrasts. Leader-driven communities, with their structured approach, can provide clear direction and facilitate goal-oriented engagement. However, their dependence on leadership for sustenance and evolution poses inherent risks, especially if the community drive is solely the responsibility of the leader, and if the leader's drive is excessive, this may be even harmful. On the other hand, organically formed communities, driven by member interaction and shared interests, exhibit a more genuine and varied engagement. Yet, these communities may lack the sustained momentum or direction often provided by a formal leadership structure.

A practical illustration of this difference can be observed in the context of a global tech company. A leader-driven community established for remote workers set objectives and organize activities, fostering a sense of purpose and direction. However, it was the spontaneously formed sub-groups within this community, centered around specific interests like coding or digital art, that displayed a remarkable burst of creativity and engagement. These sub-groups, though lacking formal structure, thrived on the authentic connections and shared passions of their members.

In remote work settings, where physical interactions are limited, the synthesis of structured leadership and organic evolution within communities can yield a harmonious balance. This approach acknowledges the value of both strategic direction and spontaneous, member-driven growth in fostering collaboration, innovation, and a sense of community in the digital domain. Recognizing the unique attributes and contributions of both types of communities is crucial in understanding the dynamics of digital collaboration and community building in contemporary remote work environments.

In my experience, blending the discussed approaches yields the best results. During onboarding interviews, we pinpoint individuals with a passion for and experience in community building. After they join, we outline our vision for the types of communities we would like to see flourishing organically within the organization. We then entrust these community-driven initiatives to these new members, who, crucially, do not bear the formal title of "community lead." This strategy allows for the organic growth and nurturing of communities, guided subtly by individuals embedded within the organization, fostering a more authentic and member-driven community culture.

I consider this blended approach as the birth of a new and modern community creation concept. This approach synergizes the strategic direction offered by leader-driven communities with the spontaneity and member-driven engagement found in organic communities.

This strategy allows for the organic development of communities, driven by the interests and passions of members but underpinned by an underlying strategic direction. It creates a symbiotic relationship where structured guidance supports the natural evolution of member-driven communities. This approach not only enhances engagement and innovation but also fosters a sense of ownership and belonging among members. It encourages a culture where ideas can emerge from the bottom up, benefiting from strategic alignment and support from the top down.

Blending leader-driven and organic community structures presents a holistic and effective approach to community building within organizations. It capitalizes on the strengths of both structured guidance and spontaneous member engagement, leading to communities that are purposeful, vibrant, and deeply resonant with their members' interests and passions.

Our collective strength as individuals is significantly amplified when we come together, whether as families, teams, or broader communities, particularly when united by common goals. This idea that "Our power as individuals is multiplied when we gather together as families, teams, and communities with common goals" resonates deeply in the context of remote teams and gig-freelancer communities. It speaks to the potential for extraordinary achievements when diverse individuals collaborate, driven by shared aspirations and purposes.

A prominent figure in spiritual philosophy and the New Age movement, David Spangler, said that "True community requires commitment and openness and a willingness to extend yourself to encounter and know the other," which is particularly pertinent in remote settings. This insight underscores the importance of commitment and openness in nurturing genuine connections and understanding within a community. It is a reminder that successful communities are not just about collective work; they are about creating spaces where people feel safe to share, learn, and grow together.

American humorist and author Leo Rosten's perspective that "The purpose of life is not to be happy, but to matter, to be productive, to be useful, to have it make some difference that you have lived at all" highlights the deeper purpose behind our communal efforts. It is not merely about individual happiness or success; it is about making a meaningful impact, contributing to something larger than ourselves, and leaving a legacy through our community involvement.

These insights guided my approach to leading remote teams and gig-freelancer communities. By embracing these philosophies, we can create more than just groups of individuals working together; we can build communities that are rich in purpose, connection, and a shared sense of making a difference. This, in essence, is what turns our professional endeavors into a fulfilling and impactful journey.

In leading remote teams and gig-freelancer communities, I have always placed special attention on building and fostering the community concept, constantly seeking ways to innovate it. If we follow the wisdom encapsulated in the words of renowned leaders, we can uncover profound insights into the essence and power of communities.

In wrapping up this crucial section, I will share a few examples of community-building exercises that we have successfully implemented. While these specific examples might not seamlessly fit into your unique environment, they could serve as a valuable source of inspiration. My hope is that these examples will spark ideas for you to consider, adapt, and experiment with within your own setting.

Problem-solving groups

The concept of "problem-solving groups" in remote and gig-freelancing setups is a strategic tool for community building uniquely suited to the challenges of these modern work environments. Distinct from real-time groups, these problem-solving groups might not assemble immediately, but they are dedicated to fostering collaboration and innovation for specific, often complex, issues.

In remote or gig-freelancing scenarios, these groups come together to tackle specific challenges or projects, bringing together individuals with the relevant skills and expertise needed to find effective solutions. These groups often function over a longer period, allowing for a more thorough analysis and development of comprehensive solutions. Utilizing digital communication and collaboration tools, such as Microsoft Teams, Slack, or different project management platforms, they bridge the geographical gap between members, ensuring smooth and efficient collaboration.

The benefits of problem-solving groups in such settings are many. They offer a structured approach to tackling complex problems, leveraging the diverse skills and perspectives of their members to foster innovative and effective solutions. These groups also provide significant learning opportunities, with members sharing knowledge and gaining new skills that can be applied in future endeavors. For remote workers and freelancers, engagement in these groups helps mitigate feelings of isolation, creating a sense of belonging and connection to a larger community. Additionally, their focus on long-term, sustainable solutions is particularly valuable for addressing ongoing or multifaceted issues.

Consider an example where a digital marketing firm employs many gig workers. The firm faces a challenge in devising a fair and motivating compensation model for these workers. To address this, the firm sets up a problem-solving group consisting of a mix of gig workers, human resource professionals, and financial analysts. Over the course of several weeks, this group delves into various compensation models, analyzing their feasibility and impact on worker motivation and productivity. They gather insights from the gig workers themselves, understanding their preferences and needs, involving human resources and finance teams for input. The group also studies industry trends and benchmarks compensation models against similar organizations.

Through this collaborative effort, the group proposes a set of compensation models that are flexible, fair, and tailored to the diverse needs of gig workers. These models include performance-based incentives, tiered compensation plans based on project complexity and duration, and additional benefits like professional development opportunities. The group's recommendations not only address the immediate need for a more effective compensation model but also set a precedent for how the firm values and supports its gig workforce.

Localized gathering cofounding / encouragement

The concept of co-funding local gatherings to help build communities represents a dynamic approach to fostering community spirit, particularly in remote or gig-freelancing setups. This strategy involves hosting local events or meetups, which are financially co-funded by organizations, to create physical spaces where remote workers and freelancers can connect, collaborate, and share experiences.

In remote and gig work environments, local gatherings serve as an essential bridge connecting the digital and physical worlds. These gatherings can range from informal meetups, workshops, and networking events to more structured conferences and training sessions. The involvement of organizations in co-funding these events demonstrates a commitment to supporting their remote and gig workforce, acknowledging the importance of face-to-face interaction in building a robust community.

These gatherings offer numerous benefits. They provide a platform for networking and relationship building, helping to reduce the sense of isolation often experienced in remote work. They also facilitate knowledge sharing and skill development, as attendees can learn from one another's experiences and insights. These events can boost morale and increase engagement, as workers feel valued and supported by their organizations. Additionally, local gatherings offer a unique opportunity for organizations to receive direct feedback from their remote workforce, fostering a culture of openness and continuous improvement.

An illustrative example of this concept can be seen in a global tech company that employs a vast network of remote workers and freelancers. The company recognizes the need for its dispersed workforce to feel connected not just virtually but also physically.

To address this, it partners with local co-working spaces and professional organizations to host quarterly meetups in various cities worldwide. These meetups feature a mix of activities, dinners, skill-building workshops, and informal networking sessions. The company co-funds these events, ensuring they are accessible to a wide range of its workforce. The gatherings become a hub for sharing best practices, discussing industry trends, building professional and personal connections, and building the desired connected communities.

Special interests groups

In the context of remote and gig-freelancing work environments, special interest groups emerge as a vital means for fostering community, offering a platform for connection and collaboration centered around shared hobbies or professional interests. Among these, a group that has the same interest in cycling can serve as an example of how such communities bring together individuals with common passions, transcending the typical work-related interactions.

In remote and gig work settings, where day-to-day interactions are primarily digital, special interest groups like a cycling community provide a unique and engaging way for individuals to connect. This cycling group would be formed of enthusiasts who share a love for sport, whether they are seasoned cyclists or new to the activity. The group's activities could range from discussing cycling techniques and gear to sharing routes and organizing virtual or in-person cycling events.

The benefits of a special cycling group are many. It creates a sense of community and belonging, counteracting the isolation that can sometimes accompany remote work. The group becomes a source of motivation and encouragement for physical fitness, which is especially important given the sedentary nature of many remote jobs. Additionally, it offers opportunities for networking and building relationships beyond professional scopes, enriching the overall work experience.

Imagine a tech company that employs remote workers globally. To support community building, the company encourages the formation of special interest groups through its internal communication platform. A group of cycling enthusiasts comes together, creating a space where they share cycling tips, favorite biking trails, and experiences. They organize weekend virtual meetups to discuss their cycling adventures and sometimes coordinate regional in-person rides.

In one innovative initiative, the group decides to organize a global virtual cycling event, where members from distinct parts of the world cycle in their local areas simultaneously and share their experiences in real time through a video call. This event not only fosters a sense of global connectivity among the members but also promotes health and wellness. The enthusiasm and participation in this event leads the company to recognize the value of such special interest groups in building a vibrant, interconnected community.

Member spotlight

The concept of a member spotlight in remote or gig-freelancing environments is an innovative approach to community building designed to enhance visibility and connectivity among community members. This strategy involves regularly featuring a member of the community, highlighting their background, achievements, hobbies, expertise, and passions. Doing so every few days or on a set schedule ensures a continual focus on different individuals within the community.

In the often dispersed and virtual world of remote and gig work, where personal interactions are limited, a member spotlight serves as a powerful tool to bridge the gap between professional and personal environments. It provides a platform for members to share their stories, showcasing the diversity of talents, interests, and experiences within the community. This practice not only fosters a sense of individual recognition but also enhances mutual understanding and respect among members.

The benefits of implementing a member spotlight feature are substantial. It helps in building a more cohesive and inclusive community by celebrating the uniqueness of each member. Such spotlights can spark conversations and connections over shared interests or experiences that might otherwise remain undiscovered in a remote setting. It also encourages knowledge sharing as members become aware of the skills and expertise within their community, potentially leading to collaborations and mentorship opportunities. Furthermore, this practice boosts morale and engagement, as members feel valued and seen by their peers and the organization.

An example of this concept in action can be drawn from a digital marketing agency with a large remote workforce. To enhance community engagement, the agency introduces a bi-weekly member spotlight feature on its internal social platform. Each spotlight includes an interview with the featured members, discussing their professional journey and personal hobbies. One spotlight, for instance, features a graphic designer who is also an avid mountain biker. This revelation leads to connections with other cycling enthusiasts within the company, sparking discussions and the formation of a cycling special interest group. Another spotlight on a project manager who volunteers in local community development projects inspires other members to share their volunteering experiences, leading to the agency organizing a company-wide volunteer day.

These spotlights not only bring to light the diverse backgrounds and interests of the agency's members but also create opportunities for deeper connections and collaborations. They contribute to a culture where everyone's story is valued, enhancing the sense of belonging and community within the remote workforce.

Gamification of skills trading

The concept of gamifying skills trading in remote and gig-freelancing communities is a creative and engaging approach to community building. This idea revolves around members registering their various skills, both professional and personal, on a common platform. Other community members interested in learning these skills can then trade their own skills in exchange. This exchange takes place in their private time and space, and afterward, participants are encouraged to share their experiences with the community, providing inspiration and motivation for others.

Gamifying skills trading serves as a unique way to connect people, foster skill development, and build a sense of community. By turning skill exchange into a game, it adds an element of fun and competition, encouraging more members to participate.

The benefits of this approach are multifaceted. It creates a dynamic environment for continuous learning and development, as members get the opportunity to acquire new skills that they might not have had access to otherwise. This trading of skills also fosters networking and builds stronger relationships within the community, as members interact on a one-on-one basis, sharing knowledge and experiences. Additionally, by sharing stories about their skill-trading experiences, members contribute to a culture of sharing and inspiration, motivating others to engage in similar exchanges.

An illustrative example of this concept can be envisioned in a large consultancy firm employing remote workers worldwide. The firm introduces a skills trading platform where employees can list skills they are willing to teach; these could range from technical skills like coding or graphic design to soft skills like public speaking or even hobbies like cooking or yoga. Employees interested in learning a new skill can browse through this list and propose a skill trade to the relevant person.

For instance, a software developer proficient in a specific programming language could offer to teach it to a colleague, who in return might teach the developer advanced Excel skills. After their trading sessions, both participants share their experiences on the company's internal social network, highlighting what they learned and how the exchange benefited them both professionally and personally. This sharing sparks interest among other employees, leading to an increase in participation in the skills trading game. The platform becomes not just a tool for learning but also a space for building connections and fostering a sense of camaraderie and mutual support within the remote community.

Friday TED Talks

TED Talks, renowned for their inspiring and informative short lectures, offers a unique platform for experts and thought leaders from various fields to share their insights, experiences, and ideas in a concise and engaging format. These talks, typically spanning up to 18 minutes, are designed to disseminate powerful ideas in a format that is both accessible and captivating to a global audience. The success and popularity of TED Talks lie in their ability to distill complex concepts into digestible, thought-provoking presentations that ignite conversations and foster learning. With this in mind, the initiative of Friday TED Talks within remote and gig-freelancing communities we work with harnesses the spirit of shared learning and personal development, making it an excellent tool for community building. This concept involves community members giving short, TED Talk-style presentations on topics they are knowledgeable or passionate about. These sessions, ideally held on Fridays, provide a platform for speakers to share interesting insights and knowledge with their peers. The duration of these talks is capped at 30 minutes, encouraging conciseness and focus.

In the context of remote or gig work, Friday TED Talks offer a valuable space for expression and connection. These sessions not only facilitate learning and knowledge sharing within the community but also provide a supportive environment for speakers to refine their public speaking skills. Receiving feedback from fellow community members, whom they regard as family members, ensures that the feedback environment is constructive and safe.

The benefits of this practice extend across several dimensions. For the speakers, it is an opportunity to refine their presentation and communication skills, gain confidence in public speaking, and receive supportive feedback from a familiar audience. For the audience members, these talks serve as a source of learning and inspiration, exposing them to innovative ideas and perspectives. Furthermore, these sessions enhance the sense of community and belonging as members come together to support and learn from one another.

An illustrative example of this could be a multinational corporation with remote employees across different continents. The corporation sets up a virtual Friday TED Talks series, where every Friday, a different employee presents a topic of their choice. These talks cover a wide range of subjects, from professional development tips and industry insights to personal interests like travel experiences or cultural topics.

For instance, one session might feature a marketing expert discussing the latest trends in digital marketing, while another Friday could have workers sharing their journey of learning a new language and the cultural insights they gained. After each talk, there is a Question & Answer session, followed by a feedback round where the audience offers constructive comments and appreciation.

The series becomes a much-anticipated weekly event within the company, with workers eagerly signing up either to speak or to listen. It not only becomes a platform for learning but also a space where employees feel seen and heard, fostering a stronger sense of community and belonging.

Fail parties
The concept of fail parties is a refreshingly candid and impactful approach to community building in remote and gig-freelancing environments. These are sessions where community members, including managers and leaders, openly share a failure they have experienced in their personal or professional lives, along with the

lessons they learned from it. By limiting the sessions to a maximum of 30 minutes, the discussions remain focused and engaging.

In the often polished and success-oriented world of professional work, especially in remote and gig settings where achievements are frequently highlighted, fail parties introduce a space for vulnerability and authenticity. This practice encourages individuals to discuss their mistakes and setbacks openly, creating a culture that values learning from failure as much as celebrating success.

The benefits of hosting fail parties are profound. Firstly, they help in fostering a culture of humbleness and empathy within the community. When leaders and managers participate, it sets a tone of openness and relatability, showing that everyone, regardless of their position, encounters and overcomes challenges. These sessions also contribute to building trust among community members, as sharing vulnerabilities is a powerful way to connect on a human level. Moreover, discussing failures and the lessons learned can be incredibly educational, providing valuable insights that others can apply in their own professional or personal lives.

Imagine a scenario in a software development company that works with a large remote team. The company introduces monthly fail parties, where team members, including senior leaders, share instances where they faced significant challenges or setbacks. For example, a project manager might share a story about a project that went off course due to poor communication and the steps they later took to improve their communication strategies. Another session could feature a developer discussing a coding error that led to a significant bug and how it taught them the importance of thorough testing and peer review.

These sessions are conducted in a relaxed and supportive atmosphere, encouraging others to ask questions and offer their perspectives. The stories shared in these fail parties not only humanize the speakers but also provide practical learnings and insights. Over time, the team begins to view failures not as a source of embarrassment but as valuable learning opportunities, fostering a more resilient and adaptive work culture.

Job market channels

The creation of dedicated channels for sharing professional and job opportunities is a strategic and community-oriented approach to fostering collaboration and support within remote and gig-freelancing environments. This concept involves setting up specific communication channels, such as forums, chat groups, or bulletin boards, where community members can post and share various job and gig opportunities they come across. These opportunities could range from remote gigs in their own countries to international freelance projects, providing a broad spectrum of options for community members.

In remote and gig work settings, where individuals often navigate their career paths independently, having access to a communal resource like this can be incredibly beneficial. It not only helps members find new opportunities but also reinforces a sense of community and mutual support. The benefits of this approach are multi-dimensional. Firstly, it provides a tangible resource for professional growth, helping members access opportunities they might not have found on their own. It also fosters a spirit of generosity and collaboration as members actively help each other advance in their careers. Additionally, such a channel can become a hub for networking and building professional relationships as members interact, discuss, and share insights about different opportunities. Moreover, for those new to the remote or gig economy, this channel can be an invaluable guide and support system, helping them navigate the landscape more effectively.

For example, in a community of freelance graphic designers, the participants can set up a dedicated Slack channel where members can share job postings, freelance project opportunities, and even requests for collaborations on larger projects. For instance, a member might post about a remote gig opportunity with a startup looking for branding and design work, which would be ideal for designers specializing in that area. Another member might share an opportunity for a collaborative project that requires a team of designers, opening the door for members to work together and pool their talents. The channel also becomes a space where members share tips on how to apply for these opportunities, discuss rates and contracts, and offer advice based on their own experiences.

Over time, this channel fosters an intense sense of community and shared purpose. Members feel supported in their professional endeavors and are more willing to contribute their own findings and insights, knowing they are part of a community that values mutual assistance and collaboration.

Mi casa es tu casa (my home is your home)

The final illustration of community fostering that resonated most with me was in a remote gig team I worked with. Here, the gig workers embraced an innovative idea titled "My home is your home." This concept revolved around a unique exchange of personal spaces. Team members openly shared details about their homes, including location, features, and photographs, in a communal platform. The essence of this initiative was to seek opportunities for house swapping with fellow gig workers, coordinating these exchanges on mutually convenient dates. This practice not only fostered a sense of community but also added an intriguing layer of personal connection and trust among the team, transcending traditional professional boundaries.

This approach surpasses typical professional interactions, venturing into a domain of personal trust and connection seldom explored in standard work environments. By opening their homes to one another, team members forge a unique bond anchored in mutual trust and respect. This practice allows them to immerse themselves in each other's lives more intimately, fostering a deeper understanding and appreciation for diverse cultures, lifestyles, and personal backgrounds.

My home is your home concept yields profound benefits. Sharing one's personal space with a colleague is an act of significant trust and vulnerability, leading to stronger, more personal connections than typical professional interactions. For teams spread across various geographic locations, this initiative provides a rich opportunity for cultural exchange, broadening members' worldviews. It also presents a practical and cost-effective way for team members to travel and explore new places, making it especially appealing in a gig economy where such opportunities can be rare. Furthermore, this practice creates a sense of belonging and community that is both unique and deeply rooted in personal experiences.

Engaging in this kind of exchange requires a high level of openness and a strong existing foundation of trust within the team. It proves the strength of the community built that such an initiative was not only proposed but embraced enthusiastically.

4. All Hearts meetings

Over the span of my career, I have experienced a variety of company cultures, ranging from those without any all-hands meetings to those organizing annual end-of-year gatherings and even some holding monthly business update meetings. The frequency and style of these meetings varied depending on the company and its leadership approach. During these sessions, vital information such as key company milestones, financial outcomes, competitive landscapes, and future projections were typically shared. Many of these meetings, however, failed to inspire me, and I consistently believed that they represented a missed opportunity to motivate and uplift the individuals in attendance. On numerous occasions, I remember being logged in through tools like Microsoft Teams but not fully engaging, often finding myself multitasking instead of paying attention.

When I began leading remote teams, I made a conscious decision to break away from the practices I had observed. In doing so, I intentionally rebranded these gatherings from **All Hands** meetings to **All Hearts** meetings. In all the organizations I have been familiar with, the term **headcount** was commonly used to refer to individual workers. I made a deliberate shift to refer to it as **heartcount** instead, too.

In this new landscape of work, the traditional terminology and practices of the corporate world are due for a significant transformation. Two such changes, the shift from All Hands meetings to All Hearts meetings and the rephrasing of headcount to heartcount, are not mere semantic adjustments. They represent a fundamental shift in organizational culture and approach, aligning more closely with the evolving nature of work and worker relationships.

The transition from All Hands to All Hearts is a powerful one. Traditionally, All Hands meetings have been about disseminating information, often focusing on operational and strategic updates, mostly numbers and often boring. While these aspects remain important, the All Hearts approach recognizes that in a remote and freelance-driven world, emotional connection and engagement are fundamental. This shift acknowledges that workers are contributing not just with their labor but also with their passion, creativity, and commitment. In an environment where physical presence is limited, fostering a sense of belonging and connection becomes crucial for productivity and morale. All Hearts meetings are, therefore, designed to be more inclusive, engaging, and empathetic, focusing on building a community and connecting with everyone on a deeper level.

Similarly, the change from headcount to heartcount speaks a lot about the evolving principles in workplaces. The term headcount reduces individuals to mere numbers, emphasizing quantity over quality. In contrast, heartcount conveys a recognition of each employee's unique value, aspirations, and emotional investment. It is a term that resonates with respect, care, and acknowledgment of the human aspect of work. In a gig economy, where workers might feel like replaceable parts of a machine, being counted as **hearts** can foster a sense of individual significance and belonging.

This linguistic evolution is crucial for several reasons:

Building trust and loyalty

Freelancers and remote workers can often feel disconnected and undervalued. By emphasizing the heart, organizations can build deeper trust and loyalty, which is essential for long-term collaboration and retention.

Enhancing engagement

Engaged workers are more productive and innovative. When people feel that they are valued not just for their output but for their whole selves, their level of engagement and commitment to the organization's goals increases.

Attracting talent

As the competition for skilled freelancers intensifies, organizations that demonstrate a genuine concern for their workers' well-being will be more attractive. Talented individuals are more likely to gravitate towards workplaces that value them as people, not just as workers.

Cultural resonance

In a world increasingly focused on mental health and work-life balance, a culture that emphasizes the heart resonates more with contemporary societal values. This alignment can enhance an organization's reputation and brand.

Inclusivity and diversity

A heart-centric approach is inherently more inclusive, recognizing the diverse needs, backgrounds, and contributions of all workers.

As the landscape of work shifts towards more remote and freelance arrangements, the move towards a more heart-centered approach in language and practice is not just a trend but a necessity. It reflects a deeper understanding of the human aspect of work, fostering a culture where individuals feel genuinely valued and connected, irrespective of their physical location or contractual terms. This shift is a step towards building more resilient, adaptive, and human-centric organizations, ready to thrive in the future of work.

Initially, in the organizations I led, All Hearts meetings were held monthly. However, we fine-tuned this schedule based on feedback from participants, finding that the most effective frequency was every two months.

In our All Hearts remote calls, we cover a variety of topics, selectively choosing a few for each meeting based on their relevance and importance rather than discussing all of them at once:

High-level operational and financial outcomes

Discuss the organization's operational strategies and financial health. Providing insights into these areas helps workers understand the broader business context and how their roles impact the organization's success.

Team impact

Spotlight the crucial role our teams play in the organization's success and in enriching our customers' experiences. This part of the meeting celebrates key team achievements and their positive effects on customers, emphasizing the real-world impact of our collective efforts and reinforcing the value of each team member's work.

Recognition and celebrations

Acknowledge individual and team achievements, milestones, or unique contributions. Recognizing hard work and success in a public forum to boost morale and show that the organization values its workers.

Personal and professional growth opportunities
Discuss new learning and development resources, upskilling programs, or pathways for career advancement. Highlighting these opportunities to motivate workers by showing commitment to their growth.

Organizational updates and future vision
Share insights into the organization's performance, future projects, and strategic direction. This helps remote and gig workers feel connected to the larger mission and understand how their work contributes to the organization's goals.

Success stories and case studies
Share stories of how challenges were overcome, either by individuals or teams. This not only provides practical insights but also inspires and motivates the participants.

Diversity and inclusion initiatives
Discuss initiatives and policies that promote diversity and inclusion within the organization. Highlighting these efforts reinforces a culture of respect and equality.

Technology and tool updates
Provide information and updates about new tools, technologies, or updates that are being introduced to improve work efficiency and collaboration.

Well-being and mental health
Address topics related to work-life balance, mental health resources, and stress management strategies. This demonstrates an understanding of the challenges remote workers face and a commitment to their overall well-being.

Feedback and open discussion forum
Encourage open communication by inviting feedback, suggestions, and ideas. This is done through Q&A sessions, interactive polls, or open discussions. Such inclusiveness makes workers feel heard and valued.

Networking and community building
Create opportunities for workers to connect with each other, share experiences, and build a sense of community. This is done through virtual breakout rooms, team-building activities, or informal chat sessions.

5. The human library

Drawing inspiration from the concept of the Human Library Organization[32], we have adopted the unique idea of creating a library of individuals. This library is designed to offer their wealth of experience and knowledge to the global gig-freelancer workforce.

Picture a library, not of books, but of people, a place where, instead of borrowing printed volumes, you borrow human beings for a conversation. These human books are individuals from diverse backgrounds, each a repository of unique experiences and knowledge. It is an idea that transcends the traditional concept of a library, turning it into a living, breathing forum for sharing and learning.

Now, envision this concept applied within the remote gig-freelancer workforce. In this setting, the library is a global network comprising individuals from various fields and specializations. Each person brings to the table their unique skills, knowledge, and life experiences, creating a rich variety of learning opportunities. This human library breaks down geographical barriers, enabling freelancers from across the world to borrow these human books and engage in meaningful conversations and knowledge exchange.

The essence of this initiative is to foster a culture of learning and knowledge sharing within the gig economy. It is an acknowledgment that every individual, regardless of their professional standing or geographic location, has something valuable to teach and an equally important capacity to learn. In a world where the gig economy is often criticized for its lack of personal connection and development opportunities, this concept emerges as a beacon of innovation and communal growth.

Let's delve deeper into the benefits and transformative potential of this initiative :

Connecting experiences and bridging gaps

The human library in the gig economy serves as a bridge connecting varied experiences and backgrounds. Freelancers often work in isolation, and this model offers a unique platform for interaction and networking. By borrowing a human book, a freelancer in New York might gain insights from a seasoned professional in Tokyo, or a budding entrepreneur in Berlin could learn from the experiences of a veteran in Silicon Valley. This exchange enriches the freelancers' professional journey, broadening their horizons beyond their immediate environment.

Fostering continuous learning and skill enhancement

In the rapidly changing gig economy, continuous learning and skill enhancement are crucial. The human library initiative allows freelancers to tap into a wealth of knowledge and expertise, helping them stay ahead in their fields. It is not just about acquiring technical skills; it is also about understanding different cultural perspectives, learning new problem-solving approaches, and gaining insights into emerging trends and technologies. This continual learning process is vital for personal and professional growth in a competitive global marketplace.

Promoting empathy and understanding

One of the most profound impacts of this concept is the promotion of empathy and understanding. By engaging with people from different walks of life, people are exposed to diverse viewpoints and life stories. This exposure can challenge preconceived notions and biases, fostering a more inclusive and empathetic approach to professional and personal interactions. In a world often divided by differences, this initiative serves as a reminder of the common human experiences that unite us.

Creating a supportive community

The gig economy can be a solitary path, but the human library concept cultivates a sense of community and belonging. It creates a support network where freelancers can seek advice, share concerns, and celebrate successes. This sense of community is vital for mental and emotional well-being, especially in a remote work setting where social interactions are limited.

Enabling personalized learning paths

Unlike traditional learning environments, the human library allows for a more personalized and flexible approach to knowledge acquisition. Freelancers can choose whom to borrow based on their specific interests, challenges, or career aspirations. This personalized approach ensures that the learning experience is relevant, engaging, and directly applicable to their professional journey.

Championing diversity and inclusion

The human library is a celebration of diversity and inclusion. It brings together people from different cultures, professions, and life experiences, offering a platform where every voice is valued and every story matters. In doing so, it not only enriches the learning experience but also fosters a more inclusive and diverse professional landscape.

The adaptation of the Human Library Organization's concept within the gig economy is more than just an innovative approach to learning and development. It represents a shift towards a more connected, empathetic, and inclusive professional world.

In our organization, we have onboarded a Human Library-like program, where we have encouraged individuals to volunteer as part of this unique project. This allowed other gig-freelancers to borrow these volunteers, much like borrowing a book from a library. We have established a comprehensive infrastructure that enables the search for these human books and facilitates their reservation for 45-minute slots. During these sessions, individuals share their experiences and knowledge. The impact of this seemingly simple yet potent initiative has been truly remarkable.

As we continue to navigate the complexities of the future of work, initiatives like this serve as powerful reminders of the limitless potential that lies in human connection and shared knowledge. For freelancers and remote workers, this is not just an opportunity to learn; it is a chance to be part of a global community that values every individual's story and contribution.

"In the pursuit of knowledge, we must remember that unlearning is often the first step to true understanding."
Albert Einstein

Personal Attributes and Development

This section emphasizes the significance of continuous self-improvement and introspection in leadership. It is about cultivating personal qualities that not only enhance one's leadership capabilities but also contribute to the overall effectiveness and resilience of the team. Leaders in remote and gig environments must focus on their self-awareness, embrace the process of unlearning outdated practices, and foster stability in their approach. This personal growth is critical in navigating the complexities of leading diverse teams. As we proceed, we will explore the importance of self-awareness, the process of unlearning, and the strategies for cultivating stability, each playing a vital role in personal and professional development.

1. Self-awareness

Self-awareness is the conscious knowledge of one's own character, feelings, motives, and desires. It involves understanding your own emotions, strengths, weaknesses, values, and drivers and how they affect others. This self-understanding enables individuals to recognize how they are perceived by others and to navigate their behavior accordingly. Being self-aware helps in making more informed decisions, developing better personal and professional relationships, and achieving a higher level of emotional intelligence. It is a critical component of personal growth and leadership, as it allows individuals to adapt, learn, and respond more effectively to different situations.

Self-awareness is a cornerstone of effective leadership as it supports several critical aspects of guiding others. Leaders who are self-aware have a clearer understanding of their own strengths, weaknesses, and biases. This deep self-knowledge enhances their decision-making, as they are more cognizant of how their preferences and predispositions influence their choices. They also communicate more effectively, adapting their message and approach to different situations and individuals, fostering a more inclusive and responsive environment.

Emotional intelligence, a byproduct of self-awareness, allows leaders to understand and manage not only their own emotions but also those of their team members, which is crucial for team cohesion and morale. Being self-aware also manifests in authenticity; such leaders are perceived as more genuine and trustworthy, which is essential for building strong, respectful relationships within the team. Furthermore, self-aware leaders are better equipped to handle conflicts constructively, as they understand their triggers and emotional responses. Lastly, self-awareness is a driver of personal growth, enabling leaders to continuously evolve and adapt, ensuring their leadership remains effective and relevant in changing circumstances.

Cultivating self-awareness begins with reflective practices, such as journaling, where you chronicle your daily experiences, thoughts, and emotions. This practice offers a deeper understanding of your inner world, like having a personal dialogue on paper. It can be guided by books like *The Artist's Way* by Julia Cameron, which introduces the concept of morning pages, a form of journaling for clarity and creativity. In the morning pages practice, you write three pages every morning about anything that comes to mind. It is not meant to be perfect or artistic, just a way to clear one's mind and get ready for the day. It is a tool for self-discovery and boosting creativity.

Mindfulness, another key aspect, involves being fully present and engaged with the here and now. It can be honed through meditation and guided by books like *Wherever You Go, There You Are* by Jon Kabat-Zinn, which offers insights into mindfulness practice. Engaging in these practices, along with seeking diverse perspectives through feedback and personal development activities, forms a comprehensive approach to developing self-awareness.

I have read several books on mindfulness, and the one I personally recommend to the reader is *Search Inside Yourself*, written by Chade-Meng Tan. In his book, Tan provides valuable insights for leaders, especially applicable to those managing remote or gig-freelancing organizations. The book emphasizes the importance of emotional intelligence and mindfulness in personal and professional success. By fostering emotional intelligence, leaders can understand themselves and others better, which is crucial for remote leadership, where face-to-face interactions are limited.

For instance, leaders who practice mindfulness, like meditation, improve their concentration, attention, and meta-attention (the heightened awareness and control over one's attentional processes, allowing an individual to not only focus but also to be aware of how and where their attention is being directed). This enhanced focus is critical in remote settings where distractions can be more prevalent and the need for deep concentration is heightened.

Self-awareness, a key component of emotional intelligence, empowers leaders to regulate their emotions and reduce negative self-talk, leading to more confident and effective leadership. This self-awareness is particularly important in remote leadership, where understanding one's emotional responses can significantly impact team dynamics and productivity.

The book highlights the effectiveness of non-material motivators, such as a sense of purpose or making a difference, which can be more challenging to convey in remote settings. By fostering a culture of happiness and purpose, leaders can motivate their remote or gig teams more effectively.

Empathy is another critical aspect. Leaders who practice empathy can build trust and understanding, which is especially important in remote teams where physical cues are absent. Empathetic leaders can better resolve conflicts and create a cohesive team environment, even when team members are geographically dispersed.

Search Inside Yourself is particularly valuable for leaders of remote or gig-freelancing teams because it focuses on developing emotional intelligence and mindfulness, skills crucial in environments where direct, face-to-face interactions are limited. The book's emphasis on self-awareness, empathy, and focused attention helps leaders navigate the unique challenges of remote leadership, such as maintaining team cohesion, effective communication, and fostering a sense of community and purpose. By applying these principles, leaders can build stronger, more resilient teams capable of thriving in the dynamic and often isolated world of remote and gig work. Tan's approach in *Search Inside Yourself* offers leaders of remote or gig-freelancing organizations a roadmap to enhance their emotional intelligence, mindfulness, and empathy. These skills are crucial for effectively managing, motivating, and supporting their teams in the increasingly prevalent remote work world. Highly recommended reading.

2. Embracing continuous learning

In an era where change is the only constant, embracing continuous learning is not just beneficial but essential. Satya Nadella, the CEO of Microsoft, champions this ideology, advocating a shift from a know-it-all to a learn-it-all attitude. This philosophy, which lies at the heart of Nadella's leadership, fosters both personal growth and organizational success.

Under Nadella's guidance, Microsoft has cultivated a culture that values continuous learning over static knowledge. The learn-it-all mindset views knowledge as an ever-evolving journey, acknowledging that there is always something new to discover, regardless of one's expertise. This approach stands in stark contrast to the know-it-all attitude, where the assumption is that one already has all the answers, leading to stagnation and a lack of openness to innovative ideas.

The advantages of adopting a learn-it-all mindset are manifold. It enhances adaptability to change, especially crucial in a world dominated by rapid technological advances, and fosters innovation, as a mindset geared towards learning encourages exploration and experimentation. Teams and individuals become more collaborative, valuing diverse perspectives and knowledge. This mindset contributes significantly to personal development, broadening one's skill set and perspectives.

Transitioning from a know-it-all to a learn-it-all mindset involves several key practices. Cultivating curiosity is fundamental, it drives the desire to learn and understand more. Viewing failures as learning opportunities rather than setbacks is crucial. This perspective, emphasized by Nadella, helps in learning from mistakes and moving forward.

Seeking and valuing feedback and constructive criticism is also important for recognizing areas for improvement. Investing time in continuous learning through various mediums, such as formal education, online courses, or workshops, is essential for staying updated and relevant.

Humility plays a significant role in this transition to the learn-it-all mindset. Acknowledging that one does not have all the answers opens doors to new learning opportunities and collaborations. In organizational settings, creating an environment that supports and encourages learning is vital. This includes providing resources and promoting knowledge sharing.

Regular reflection is another key practice. It allows for assessing what has been learned and how it can be applied, forming an integral part of the learning process. I suggest taking the time to read a book I read multiple times, titled *Ego Is the Enemy*, written by Ryan Holiday. This book is a compelling exploration of how our own egos can be a significant barrier to success and personal growth and a blocker to the learn-it-all mindset. The book delves into historical and contemporary examples, illustrating how ego has led to the downfall of many influential figures while humility has propelled others to great achievements. At its core, the book argues that ego, defined as an inflated sense of self-importance and self-obsession, is a destructive force. Holiday suggests that ego can blind us to our faults, prevent learning and growth, and lead to harmful choices. It can cause us to overestimate our abilities and underestimate challenges, leading to failure. Conversely, those who achieve lasting success and fulfillment are often marked by humility, openness to learning, and a realistic assessment of their abilities and circumstances. Connecting this to the learn-it-all mindset advocated by Satya Nadella, the parallels are evident. Holiday's emphasis on humility aligns with Nadella's encouragement for individuals to shift from a know-it-all attitude to a learn-it-all approach. Both perspectives recognize that success and growth are rooted in the ability to maintain an open, curious mind and a realistic view of oneself and the world.

The learn-it-all mindset, free from the constraints of ego, fosters a continuous quest for knowledge and improvement. It encourages embracing failure as a learning opportunity, seeking feedback, and valuing collaborative efforts, which are all practices that are hindered by a dominant ego. Thus, the principles outlined in *Ego Is the Enemy* complement the philosophy of continuous learning and adaptation, emphasizing that humility is not just a virtue but a practical approach to personal and professional development.

The shift from a know-it-all to a learn-it-all mindset is transformative. It is essential for staying relevant, fostering innovation, and achieving personal growth in a constantly changing world. By embracing a philosophy of continuous learning and openness to new experiences, individuals and organizations can unlock their full potential and drive significant progress.

Discovering the diverse talents surrounding you helps you open your eyes to a world of knowledge you never knew existed, a shift from being a know-it-all to embracing a learn-it-all attitude. This approach is especially significant when you lead a global team. Each smart individual, with unique experiences and backgrounds, contributes to a wide range of global viewpoints. Such a realization is both humbling and exhilarating. The richness of working with a team so diverse, with members coming from various cultural, professional, and personal backgrounds, transforms into a continuous learning journey. This transformation underlines the importance of remaining open and adaptable, consistently learning from the wealth of perspectives around you.

Leading a remote or gig freelancing team in this digital era requires harnessing these principles. It involves creating a culture where continuous learning is not just encouraged but integrated into the very workflow of the team. Utilizing digital tools for knowledge sharing, encouraging team members to engage in online learning, and fostering an environment of open communication and feedback are key strategies in this regard.

The journey of helping remote gig-freelancer workers from know-it-all to learn-it-all mindset was a crucial leadership challenge, but with the right strategies, we made it happen and below are some of the practices we applied:

Modeling the behavior
With the help of the leaders within the organization, we adopted a learn-it-all mindset ourselves, demonstrating our own continuous learning and openly sharing our learning journey at every opportunity. This set a powerful example for the team and showed them that learning is a lifelong process.

Promoting curiosity
Curiosity, a fundamental aspect of human psychology, plays a pivotal role in the way our brains function and develop. This innate desire to explore and understand the world around us is not just a childhood trait but a powerful force that continues to shape our cognitive processes throughout life. When we engage in acts of curiosity, such as asking questions or exploring new ideas, our brains are stimulated in unique and beneficial ways.

Neuroscientific research reveals that when we are curious, certain regions of our brain light up, particularly those associated with pleasure and reward. This response is like what happens when we experience something enjoyable, like savoring a favorite food or listening to a beloved piece of music. The neurotransmitter dopamine, often linked to feelings of happiness and satisfaction, is released during curious explorations, providing a natural boost to our mood and well-being.

Curiosity enhances our cognitive abilities. When we are curious about a subject, our brain is more likely to retain information related to it. This is because curiosity puts the brain in a state that is primed for learning. It opens the door to new neural pathways, making it easier to assimilate and recall information. Curiosity transforms the way we engage with information, turning a passive activity into an active and rewarding process.

The psychological effects of being curious extend beyond immediate pleasure and memory enhancement. Curiosity fosters a deeper level of engagement with life and work, cultivating a sense of purpose and fulfillment. It drives us to question, dive deeper, and challenge our own understanding, which is crucial for intellectual growth and personal development. In a team setting, this translates to more innovative ideas, better problem-solving skills, and a collaborative spirit, as each member brings their unique inquisitive perspectives to the table. The act of being curious has a positive impact on our emotional health. It encourages an open-minded approach to life, making us more adaptable and resilient in the face of challenges and changes. Curiosity helps in building empathy as well, as it drives us to understand perspectives different from our own, a crucial skill in both personal and professional relationships.

As someone inherently curious, I cherish this characteristic not just for my individual development, but also in molding our culture of remote work and gig-freelancing. We made it a point to cultivate curiosity within our team. We created an environment where asking questions and seeking answers was not just accepted but appreciated. We instituted regular "ask us anything" sessions, providing a platform for everyone to express their curiosity and ask questions that mattered to them. Every question was met with positivity and openness, fostering a culture of exploration and inquiry, which is fundamental to continuous learning.

Emphasizing growth
Challenges and mistakes were framed as opportunities for learning and growth. This helped to shift the focus from knowing everything to learning from every experience. It also helped to create a safe space where team members felt comfortable taking risks and trying new things. We shared instances where we believed our knowledge was superior to others, but this led to strategic failures and unexpected results. This served as a lesson for our team, demonstrating that presuming to know everything can lead to significant missteps. It also created a safe space for our

team members, showing them that it is okay not to have all the answers.

Providing resources

Learning resources were made readily available, and their use was encouraged. This included books, online courses, webinars, and mentoring programs. By providing these resources, we ensured that team members had the tools they needed to learn and grow.

Recognizing and rewarding learning

Individuals who demonstrated a commitment to learning were acknowledged. This was done through shout-outs in team meetings, awards, and other forms of recognition. We even co-funded learning and certification. This not only motivated the individuals but also inspired others in the team to engage in continuous learning.

The benefits of fostering a learn-it-all culture have been many. Team members became more engaged and motivated. They constantly improved their skills and brought new ideas to the table. This has led to increased productivity and innovation. This culture has made our team more resilient. With the rapid pace of technological change, the ability to learn and adapt is crucial. Our team members are not only equipped to deal with change, but they also see it as an opportunity to learn and grow. Interestingly, this culture has also made our team more attractive to gig-freelancers.

In the gig economy, the ability to learn and adapt is key to staying up-to-date. By offering a culture that values and promotes continuous learning, we can attract talented freelancers who are eager to learn and grow.

In conclusion, fostering a learn-it-all culture in a remote or gig freelancing team is not just beneficial but essential in the digital era. It requires a shift in mindset, the right strategies, and a commitment to continuous learning. But the benefits, increased engagement, productivity, innovation, resilience, and attractiveness to freelancers, make it all worthwhile.

3. Unlearning

Learning new things is often celebrated as a standard of progress and adaptability. This pursuit of knowledge, like the constant evolution seen in academic fields or the iterative advancements in technology, is a shared trait among many successful individuals. However, the less heralded yet equally crucial counterpart to learning is unlearning. Unlearning, in its essence, is the process of discarding outdated or incorrect information and practices, much like scientists must abandon old theories in light of new evidence or how software engineers deprecate legacy code to make way for more efficient, modern solutions.

The challenge of unlearning is steeped in its complexity. It is not merely about forgetting; it is about actively breaking down ingrained habits and long-held beliefs like a historian critically re-examining established narratives in the light of new historical discoveries. This process often involves stepping back to view the bigger picture.

Unlearning becomes a pivotal skill within the context of remote work or gig-freelancing. For many, this shift requires a paradigmatic change in thinking, challenging the traditional office-centric model of work. It is a cognitive leap comparable to the transition from analog to digital technologies, where old protocols give way to new methodologies. Data and research support the significance of unlearning in adapting to rapid change. Multiple studies highlight that professionals who actively engage in unlearning outdated practices adapt more effectively to change and innovation.

The heart-brain division in unlearning is particularly intriguing. While the heart clings to the comfort of the known and the traditional, the brain recognizes the necessity to unlearn for progress. This internal conflict mirrors the tension between classical and quantum physics, where new paradigms do not easily replace established ones but are essential for further advancement.

Addressing the question of whether humans can adapt as fast as technology evolves, the answer lies in our ability to unlearn. Just as software systems are updated to stay relevant, so must our thought processes be continually revised.

Leading others in a remote or gig-freelancer setup toward unlearning is as challenging as it is essential. It is about guiding a team to adopt new knowledge and to shed obsolete practices and ideas. This leadership in unlearning, much like a conductor harmonizing an orchestra with a blend of old and new compositions, requires patience, empathy, and a clear vision.

A book that would be particularly useful for practicing unlearning is *Think Again: The Power of Knowing What You Don't Know* by Adam Grant. Adam Grant, an organizational psychologist, delves into the importance of rethinking and unlearning in personal and professional life. The book emphasizes the value of questioning one's own beliefs and opinions and being open to new ideas and perspectives. It is an insightful read for anyone looking to improve their ability to adapt, learn, and unlearn in a rapidly changing world. Grant uses a blend of research, storytelling, and practical advice to guide readers through the process of unlearning and re-evaluating their assumptions and beliefs. This book is particularly beneficial for leaders, managers, and professionals who need to navigate complex, dynamic environments, much like those in remote and gig-freelancer work settings. It offers strategies for fostering a culture of learning and unlearning within organizations, making it a valuable resource for anyone interested in enhancing their adaptability and cognitive flexibility.

In my leadership career, shaped by the wisdom of invaluable mentors, I have discovered the transformative power of unlearning. This journey began with a conscious shift in mindset, recognizing that unlearning is as vital as learning in navigating the complexities of modern leadership. Through various practices, I have harnessed the benefits of unlearning, which have been instrumental in my professional growth and adaptability. I have regularly engaged in reflective practice, dedicating time to deeply questioning my knowledge and beliefs. This self-examination has often led to profound insights, revealing biases and outdated ideas that needed discarding. It is like sifting through a treasure trove of experiences, discerning which gems of wisdom to keep and which to let go of. I have actively sought diverse perspectives, stepping out of my comfort zone to engage with thoughts and ideas different from my own. This practice has been like opening windows in a room long closed, letting in fresh air and new lights. It challenged my preconceptions and broadened my understanding of complex issues.

Embracing failure as a learning opportunity has been pivotal. I have learned to view failures not as setbacks but as stepping stones to greater understanding and resilience. Analyzing my failures has often illuminated paths to unlearning and relearning, leading to improved strategies and approaches. Questioning assumptions has been a regular exercise in my leadership toolkit. I have learned to probe the foundations of my beliefs, asking why I hold them and considering the validity of beliefs contrary to my own. This practice has been crucial in shedding outdated modes of thinking and adopting more effective contemporary views.

My curiosity has been a guiding light, driving me to explore and learn continuously. It is a thirst for knowledge that goes beyond traditional learning, encompassing the unlearning of obsolete information and practices. Practicing mindfulness and self-awareness, whether being through 15 minutes of daily meditation, maintaining a daily reflective journal, or exercising gratitude every day, has helped me recognize my automatic thoughts and behaviors. This awareness has been key in identifying areas where unlearning was necessary, facilitating a more adaptive and responsive leadership style. My commitment to continuous learning has naturally led to the unlearning of outdated information. By staying up to date on the latest trends and developments, I have kept my knowledge base relevant and effective. Experimentation and exploration have been a part of my leadership principles. Challenging conventional wisdom and trying innovative approaches have often revealed better ways of doing things and highlighted areas where my previous knowledge was lacking. Seeking and valuing feedback, especially from those with differing viewpoints, has been crucial. This input has often highlighted blind spots in my understanding and prompted necessary unlearning. Throughout this journey, patience and persistence have been my allies. Unlearning is not instantaneous; it is a process that unfolds over time.

Unlearning is a critical component in adapting to and thriving in the dynamic landscape of remote and gig work. It requires a deliberate effort to shed outdated practices and embrace new paradigms, a process as complex and necessary as the evolution of academic thought or the advancement of technology. As leaders and professionals, our ability to unlearn and relearn will define our capacity to navigate and succeed in these changing times.

4. Cultivating stability

For gig-freelancers, one of the primary concerns is ensuring their ongoing involvement in projects they have committed to. This aspect of their career is not just about job security and income but also about their professional development and personal satisfaction.

Feedback plays a critical role in this context. It is not just a tool for improvement but also a means for freelancers to understand their standing and progress in a project. Nonetheless, there is another aspect that holds equal importance: empathetic recognition by leaders of freelancers and gig workers' concerns about stability, especially in a remote working environment. Empathy goes beyond mere acknowledgment of challenges. It involves a deep understanding of the freelancer's perspective, especially in the landscape of mid-to-long-term projects.

The world of gig-freelancing is marked by numerous benefits such as flexibility, exposure to diverse projects, and the opportunity for rapid skill development. Yet, it also harbors an extremely competitive environment. The global accessibility of job opportunities means that gig workers are constantly in a race to secure their next engagement. This competition can be a double-edged sword, providing opportunities but also fostering an intense and sometimes stressful work atmosphere.

In some unfortunate scenarios, I have observed managers leveraging this competitive landscape inappropriately. They practiced the threat of termination over freelancers, creating a high-pressure environment that can adversely affect both performance and mental well-being. Such tactics are not only harmful to the individual but also counterproductive to the organization's goals. A caring and effective leader approaches these situations with empathy and understanding, recognizing the unique challenges faced by freelancers.

Gig-freelancers are acutely aware of their vulnerability in the face of budget cuts or project realignments. The knowledge that they might be the first to face contract termination in such situations can foster a pervasive sense of insecurity. This fear of losing their current project can become a constant backdrop to their professional life, influencing their work and mindset.

In my experience, one effective way to mitigate these concerns is through constant and transparent communication. This involves not just updates about the project but also sharing insights about the available budget and prospects in a timely manner. Such openness helps in building trust and providing freelancers with a sense of stability and inclusion.

In instances where business demands have required the closure of certain projects, we have strived to handle the situation with a lot of care and foresight. Timely communication with the freelancers involved has been our priority.

Our approach extends beyond mere notification; we actively explore opportunities for freelancers in other ventures within our organization. This is contingent on the alignment of their skills with the new roles. In cases where a direct transition is not feasible, we seek to provide a buffer period. This grace period is crucial for freelancers, allowing them to look for new opportunities and prepare for the transition without abrupt disruption to their professional lives and, most importantly, their income. This approach underlines a broader philosophy in the gig economy, the recognition that while freelancers are independent, their success and well-being are intertwined with the practices and principles of the organizations they collaborate with. Leaders who embrace this philosophy not only contribute to the well-being of freelancers but also build a more resilient, adaptable, and committed workforce. In an environment that is increasingly defined by remote work and project-based engagements, such practices are not just beneficial; they are essential for fostering a sustainable and productive work environment.

"The art of life lies in a constant readjustment to our surroundings."
Kakuzo Okakura

Harmonizing Multigenerational Talent

The emergence of remote work and gig-freelancing has fundamentally altered corporate operations. As organizations and their leaders, irrespective of size, adapt to this evolving landscape, a key aspect that emerges as a priority is the generational diversity within the workforce.

From the resilient Greatest Generation born before 1927 to the digitally native Generation Alpha born after 2013, each group brings its unique set of values, experiences, and expectations to the table. Understanding these generational differences is not just beneficial; it is essential for effective leadership in a global, remote work environment. Being intentional about this element has brought significant benefits during my leadership of remote or gig-freelancer workers by listening and communicating slightly differently after becoming conscious of this ecosystem.

Baby Boomers, who thrived in the post-war economic boom, often value stability and face-to-face communication, while Generation X, growing up in the rise of technology, shows a blend of traditional and modern work ethics. Millennials, on the other hand, are known for their tech-savviness and value flexibility and purpose in their careers. Meanwhile, Generation Z, the first to grow up entirely in the digital age, brings a whole new perspective, valuing innovation, diversity, and global thinking.

As corporations increasingly turn to a mix of remote and gig freelancers, leaders must adapt their strategies to manage, motivate, and engage a multigenerational workforce that spans different time zones, cultures, and digital platforms. In this section, the nuances of leading such a diverse group will be discussed, exploring what it takes to harmonize the strengths and preferences of different generations for corporate success in the global digital arena.

Envision leading a diverse team of 20 individuals, not only diverse in cultural backgrounds but also spanning across multiple generations. This scenario, while challenging, is increasingly common in today's global work environment. As you apply the leadership practices outlined in this book, leveraging your innate qualities of empathy and care, it is crucial to also be mindful of the generational dynamics at play.

Each generation, from Baby Boomers to Generation Alpha, brings its distinct perspectives, work ethics, and communication styles. As a leader, recognizing and addressing these nuances will be key to fostering a harmonious and productive team. Additionally, it is important to be self-aware of your own generational biases and preferences, as they can subtly influence your leadership approach. By being cognizant of these factors, you can better navigate the complexities of leading a multigenerational team in a remote or gig work setting.

This book does not focus on examining generational gaps. However, as a leader in any sizable organization, you are likely to face these differences, whether you are conscious of them or not.

My goal is to raise awareness about this issue and share my insights and experiences, along with relevant background information, which I think you will find valuable.

As I mentioned in different sections of this book, the shift towards remote work and the gig economy has been significant, especially in the wake of global events such as the COVID-19 pandemic. Companies have had to adapt quickly, transitioning from in-person to virtual environments. This change has brought to light the challenges and opportunities of managing a workforce that is not only physically dispersed but also generationally diverse.

The key to successful leadership in this context lies in flexibility and adaptability. Leaders must be willing to tailor their communication and management styles to suit the needs of their team members. This might mean adopting modern technology platforms for younger generations or ensuring more traditional methods of communication and feedback for older generations. It also involves creating an inclusive culture that respects and values the contributions of all generations.

The Baby Boomers, born between 1946 and 1964, grew up during a time of post-war prosperity and social change. They are often ambitious, with a strong work ethic. In a remote setting, they may prefer more direct forms of communication, like phone calls or emails, and value recognition for their experience and contributions. They can be encouraged to coach younger members, and they would be immensely proud and exceptionally good at it. In our organization we implemented this practice years ago, and it has shown to be extremely successful.

Generation X, born between 1965 and 1980, witnessed the emergence of personal computing and the Internet. They are generally independent, resourceful, and skeptical of authority. Flexibility and work-life balance are important to them. In a remote work environment, they tend to be adaptable, preferring a mix of traditional and digital communication methods. I am part of this category, and this explains my passion for flexibility and the ability to bridge older generations to the younger ones.

Millennials, born between 1981 and 1996, are digital natives who value flexibility, collaboration, and innovation. They are comfortable with technology and often seek work that provides a sense of purpose. For managing Millennials remotely, leaders should focus on clear, concise digital communication and offer opportunities for growth and development. My learning from millennials has been immense, particularly their innovative spirit. In the communities we have established, we have consciously utilized their energy and ambition for progress and success.

Generation Z, the first generation to grow up entirely in the digital age, is entering the workforce now. Born between 1997 and 2012, they are true digital natives, adept at multitasking and comfortable with an array of digital platforms. They value inclusivity, diversity, and social responsibility. In a remote setting, engaging with them through various digital channels and providing regular feedback and collaboration opportunities can be effective. This generation is our world's immediate future, and learning from them and preparing them properly has been fundamental in the organizations I have led so far.

Now let us discuss the challenges a leader might face within this ecosystem:

Leading a multigenerational remote team presents a unique set of challenges stemming from the differing values, communication preferences, and work styles of each generation. The complexities of managing such a team are heightened in a remote setting, where physical cues are absent, and digital communication is paramount.

One of the primary challenges is communication barriers. Each generation has its preferred mode of communication, ranging from traditional phone calls and emails favored by Baby Boomers and Generation X to the instant messaging and social media platforms popular with Millennials and Generation Z. These preferences can lead to misunderstandings or disconnects if not managed effectively.

Motivational drivers also vary significantly across generations. While older generations might value job security and financial incentives, younger generations often seek meaningful work, personal growth opportunities, and a positive impact on society. This divergence requires leaders to adopt varied engagement strategies that cater to the motivational needs of each group.

Technological adaptability is another crucial factor. While younger generations are typically comfortable with rapidly changing technology, older generations might have a steeper learning curve. This disparity can affect how different age groups adapt to and embrace remote work tools and practices.

Potential generational biases and conflicts can arise in a multigenerational team. Misunderstandings stemming from different work ethics, communication styles, or resistance to change can lead to friction. Leaders need to be aware of these biases, both in themselves and within their teams, and work proactively to foster understanding and respect among team members.

To effectively lead a multigenerational remote team, leaders must, therefore, be skilled in communication, adaptable in their management approaches, and sensitive to the diverse needs of their team members. By recognizing and addressing the unique challenges posed by generational differences, leaders can harness the strengths of each group to build a more dynamic, collaborative, and productive remote workforce.

In my experience leading such teams for years, my team and I have implemented some practices to communicate effectively with each generation and to create common ground. Here are some things we implemented directly or indirectly:

Using a variety of communication tools

We incorporated a mix of communication methods, including emails, phone calls, video conferencing, instant messaging, and collaboration platforms like Microsoft Teams. This approach ensured that everyone's preferences were considered.

Regular and structured check-ins

We scheduled regular check-ins with the team and one-on-one meetings with individuals. This helped bridge communication gaps and provided a platform for addressing concerns and sharing updates.

Clear and concise communication

Regardless of the medium used, we ensured that all communication is clear, concise, and jargon-free. This approach is universally appreciated across generations. We conducted many surveys on our communication style and aligned it to the feedback provided by the team members representing different generations.

Encourage cross-generational collaboration

We created projects or teams that included members from different generations. This fostered understanding and appreciation of diverse perspectives and work styles. Initially, in some instances, we saw friction, but once we explained the purpose of the collaboration, which was to understand each other and, most importantly, to learn, things went well.

Provide training and support

As much as we could and as the budget allowed, we offered training sessions for new software or communication tools, business models, and concepts such as AI usage in the workspace, especially for those who might be less tech-savvy or less informed. This helped level the playing field and reduced anxiety around technology use.

Empathetic leadership

To the best of our ability, we showed empathy and comprehension towards the distinct hurdles and preferences encountered by each generation. This fostered trust and facilitated open communication. Achieving this can sometimes be challenging, but with purposeful actions and patience, it is possible to yield positive results.

Feedback mechanisms

We established mechanisms for both giving and receiving feedback, making sure these methods were user-friendly and comfortable for all age groups. Despite the frequency, we never ceased to seek feedback. We initiated weekly pulse surveys consisting of brief, one or two-question formats and employed AI for comprehensive 360-degree feedback analysis. The outcomes of using AI have been remarkable, revealing patterns that went previously unnoticed.

Customize motivational strategies

We acknowledged and valued the efforts of our team members in ways that were meaningful to them. For instance, we noticed that the older generations generally preferred formal recognition, which typically involves structured and official acknowledgments such as certificates, awards, or public announcements. On the other hand, the younger generations seemed to appreciate public or peer-based recognition more. This type of recognition is often less formal and can include shout-outs in team meetings, acknowledgments in group chats, or compliments from colleagues. These methods of recognition are more public and involve the individual's peers, hence the term peer-based.

Flexibility in work hours

We offered flexible working hours, when possible, as preferences may vary widely across generations, with some valuing a strict schedule and others preferring flexibility.

Encourage knowledge sharing

We initiated mentorship and shadowing programs where older generations could share their experience and younger generations could provide tech-savvy insights. This reciprocal learning fostered mutual respect and collaboration.

Use visual aids in communication

We intentionally incorporated visual elements like infographics or short videos in communications, as we understood that they would be more engaging and easier to understand than long text documents.

Cultural sensitivity training

We provided training in cultural sensitivity and generational differences to promote a deeper understanding and respect among team members.

Accessible and inclusive language

We used language that is inclusive and free from generational stereotypes, ensuring that all communications are respectful and considerate. This topic, especially in today's world, is very sensitive, and we have been very careful and intentional about using the right language in communications.

Promote social interaction

We organized virtual social events or informal chat groups to help team members connect on a personal level beyond work-related topics. We even supported local get-together meetings so people who are geographically close enough could meet and get to know each other. Feedback on those events was extraordinary.

"Investing in tomorrow's technology today is more critical than ever."
Bill Gates

The Imperative of Technological Familiarity

As we step into the future of work, the role of leadership is evolving dramatically. This future is not confined to traditional office spaces or typical nine-to-five routines. It is a global, digital, and flexible landscape, demanding a significant shift in leadership approach, especially in their relationship with technology.

Consider the world of work as it is transforming. Offices are no longer just buildings; they are virtual spaces spanning continents. Teams are diverse, not just in skills but in locations and working hours. In this new environment, leaders are not just managers or decision-makers; they're digital pioneers. They need to understand and leverage technology not just as a tool but as a critical component of their leadership strategy.

Remote work, for instance, has opened up opportunities to engage with talent from all over the world. But leading a distributed team is more than having an internet connection and a laptop. Leaders need to be well-versed in various digital tools and platforms that support communication, collaboration, and productivity. This isn't just about knowing which buttons to click; it is about understanding how these tools can be used to maintain team cohesion and drive efficiency, regardless of physical location.

Navigating the gig economy as a leader involves a nuanced understanding of technology and its various applications in this unique work environment. The gig economy, characterized by its reliance on short and mid-term contracts and freelance work, depends heavily on digital platforms, which are central to connecting freelancers with potential opportunities. Leaders adept in this space know how to use these platforms not just to find talent but also to understand the dynamics of these digital marketplaces and how best to engage with gig workers within them. Once gig workers are brought on board, managing their contributions requires a different approach. Here, project management tools and systems come into play, offering leaders the ability to track progress, set deadlines, and share resources effectively. The key challenge lies in balancing the need for project oversight with the independence that gig workers often value. In this regard, technology serves as a bridge, facilitating communication and collaboration without impinging on the autonomy of the gig worker.

Payment processing is another crucial aspect where technology plays an integral role in the gig economy. Understanding and utilizing various digital payment platforms is essential for ensuring smooth, timely, and secure financial transactions. This not only involves the mechanics of transferring funds but also understanding the preferences and norms surrounding payments in the gig workforce.

The legal and ethical dimensions of gig work add another layer of complexity. With many of these considerations tied to technology, leaders must navigate the intricacies of data privacy, intellectual property rights, and contract enforcement in a digital context. Staying informed about legal frameworks and using technology to comply with these regulations is critical, especially when it involves handling sensitive company information.

Building relationships and fostering engagement with gig workers also presents a unique challenge in the absence of traditional office settings. In this digital landscape, leaders must employ technology creatively to establish rapport and a sense of inclusion among gig workers. Regular virtual interactions, feedback sessions, and inclusive team meetings are some ways in which leaders can use technology to create a sense of belonging and value for these workers despite the often transient nature of their engagement.

The gig economy is a dynamic and ever-evolving domain, with new platforms and tools emerging constantly. Leaders must keep their finger on the pulse of these changes, staying updated with the latest trends and innovations. This includes being aware of new platforms, evolving best practices, and technological advancements that could impact the sourcing, management, and compensation of gig work. In leading within the gig economy, the challenge for leaders is to harness technology not only for logistical management but also to create an environment that is productive, engaging, and compliant with legal and ethical standards. This demands a combination of technological proficiency, strategic foresight, and the flexibility to adapt to the ever-changing landscape of gig work. Technology has transformed communication and collaboration. It is not enough to use these tools; leaders must know how to choose and utilize them effectively. This means understanding their strengths and limitations to ensure seamless information flow and collaboration across different teams and time zones.

Innovation is another key area where technology is crucial. Leaders need to keep pace with the latest technological trends to spot opportunities for innovation and guide their teams in leveraging technology creatively. This is about fostering a culture where technology is not just used for its sake but is an enabler of new ideas and approaches.

Decision-making in today's digital age is increasingly data-driven. Leaders who understand technology can access and interpret vast amounts of data, using it to make informed, strategic decisions. This requires familiarity with data analysis tools and an understanding of how to apply this information in a business context. Making data-driven decisions in today's leadership landscape is a critical component, especially when leading a remote or gig-based workforce scattered across the globe. The digital age has blessed us with an abundance of data, but the real skill lies in the ability to harness this data effectively to make strategic decisions. This process is multifaceted, involving the collection, analysis, and interpretation of data and then applying it in a meaningful way to guide business strategies and operations. Firstly, the collection of data is an ongoing process. Leaders need to identify which data is relevant to their objectives. This could range from performance metrics of remote teams, customer feedback, and market trends to operational efficiency data. With the right tools, collecting this data is not just about accumulating numbers; it is about gathering insights that can illuminate various aspects of the business. Once the data is collected, the next step is analysis. This is where leaders must have or develop a level of proficiency in data analysis tools and techniques. These tools can help decipher complex data sets, revealing patterns, trends, and correlations that might not be apparent at first glance. For a leader, the ability to analyze data is not just about understanding graphs and charts; it is about reading the story that the data is telling. It is about looking beyond the numbers to understand what they signify in terms of business operations, employee performance, customer satisfaction, and market opportunities. Interpreting the data is perhaps the most critical step. This is where leaders transform data into actionable insights. It is not just about what the data shows but about understanding why it matters. This involves contextualizing the data within the broader scope of the business environment. Leaders must be able to connect the dots between disparate pieces of information and discern how they impact the organization's objectives. This step often requires not just analytical skills but also experience, intuition, and a deep understanding of the business. Applying the data is the final and most crucial step. Here, leaders use the insights derived from data to make informed decisions. This could involve strategic planning, resource allocation, process improvements, or adapting business models. In the context of remote and gig workforces, it could mean adjusting management practices, changing communication strategies, or introducing new tools and technologies to boost productivity and engagement. Furthermore, data-driven decision-making is not a one-off task. It is a continuous cycle of measuring, learning, and improving. Leaders need to establish systems and cultures where data is regularly reviewed and insights are acted upon. It is about creating a feedback loop where decisions are constantly informed by fresh data, leading to a culture of continual improvement and agility.

Finally, cybersecurity is a growing concern in a digital work environment. Leaders must have a basic understanding of cybersecurity to protect their organization's data and digital assets. This includes being aware of potential threats and understanding best practices for safeguarding information. Ensuring cybersecurity is a crucial aspect of modern leadership, particularly when overseeing remote teams or gig workers. With the digital transformation of workplaces, concerns such as privacy breaches, hacking, cyberattacks, data security, intellectual property protection, and secure system access become paramount. Each of these areas requires specific attention and strategies to safeguard the organization's digital assets.

Let us look at those areas one by one :

Privacy
In a remote work environment, maintaining privacy involves protecting sensitive information from unauthorized access. This is not only about securing data but also about respecting the privacy of employees and clients. Leaders must ensure that their teams use secure communication channels and that data storage and sharing practices comply with privacy laws and regulations. This often involves implementing encryption protocols and VPNs (Virtual Private Networks), along with training team members on privacy best practices and recognizing potential privacy threats.

Hacking and cyberattacks
The risk of hacking and cyberattacks is heightened in remote work settings due to the dispersed nature of the workforce and the varied networks being used. Leaders must be proactive in implementing robust security measures such as multi-factor authentication, firewalls, and anti-malware software. Regular security audits and vulnerability assessments are critical to identify and mitigate potential risks. Additionally, establishing a rapid response plan for potential breaches is vital for minimizing damage and restoring security.

Data security
Protecting the integrity and confidentiality of data is a fundamental concern. This involves ensuring that data, both at rest and in transit, is securely encrypted. Data security policies must be in place, outlining clear guidelines on data handling, storage, and sharing. Regular backups and a well-planned disaster recovery strategy are essential to prevent data loss and ensure business continuity in case of a security breach.

Intellectual property security

With remote and gig workers often involved in creative or development processes, protecting intellectual property becomes a critical responsibility. Leaders must ensure that agreements with remote and gig workers clearly define the ownership of any created intellectual property. Secure collaboration tools should be employed to protect the development process, and access to sensitive information should be strictly controlled and monitored.

Secure systems access

Providing remote and gig workers with access to company systems while ensuring that this access is secure and controlled is a challenging aspect of cybersecurity. Implementing robust access management protocols, such as role-based access controls, can help mitigate the risks. It is also important to regularly review and update access privileges, ensuring that only authorized personnel have access to sensitive systems and data. In addition to these specific areas, a culture of cybersecurity awareness within the organization is crucial. Regular training sessions on cybersecurity best practices, recognizing phishing attempts, and safe internet practices are essential in empowering employees to be the first line of defense against cyber threats. Leaders must also stay informed about the latest cybersecurity trends and threats, adapting their strategies accordingly.

Furthermore, for organizations engaging with gig workers, ensuring that these independent contractors adhere to the organization's cybersecurity standards poses a unique challenge. This often requires clear communication of expectations, regular check-ins, and potentially providing them with secure tools and software. In ensuring cybersecurity, leaders face the complex task of balancing accessibility and security. They must foster an environment where teams can collaborate and work efficiently without compromising the security of the organization's digital assets. In the evolving landscape of remote work and the gig economy, cybersecurity is not just a technical issue but a strategic imperative that requires ongoing attention, adaptation, and leadership commitment.

In summary, as the workplace becomes more digital, global, and flexible, leaders must enhance their technological familiarity. This is crucial not just for managing teams and projects but for driving innovation, making informed decisions, and ensuring the security of digital assets. The call for leaders to deepen their technological understanding is urgent and indispensable for navigating the future of work.

CONCLUSIONS

As this book concludes its exploration into the evolving dynamics of leadership in the sectors of remote, gig, and freelance work, we find ourselves on the brink of a significant shift in the work environment.

As the writer of this book, it is clear to me that organizations worldwide, regardless of size, must seriously consider the implications of remote work and the gig-freelancer workforce. Many companies are slow to recognize this shift, but the benefits of embracing a remote and gig economy are undeniable and multifaceted. Governments, too, must act swiftly to regulate and support this evolving landscape.

Remote work and gig-freelancing represent a more ecological and sustainable approach to employment. By reducing the need for physical office spaces, companies can significantly lower their carbon footprint. This reduction in office-related resource consumption and commuting translates to a tangible positive impact on the environment.

This new work paradigm offers unparalleled flexibility and agility. For employees, the ability to work from anywhere at any time fosters a better work-life balance, leading to increased job satisfaction and mental well-being. For employers, this flexibility means access to a global talent pool unrestricted by geographical boundaries. This diversity of perspectives and skills can drive innovation and creativity, leading to more dynamic and successful businesses.

Cost efficiency is another compelling advantage. Remote work and gig freelancing can lead to substantial savings on overhead costs such as office space, utilities, and equipment. These savings can be redirected to other strategic investments, further driving company growth and stability.

Beyond these tangible benefits, remote work and gig freelancing can enhance organizational resilience. In a world where change is the only constant, the ability to adapt quickly is crucial. A remote and flexible workforce can respond more rapidly to market changes and global events, ensuring business continuity under various circumstances.

The shift towards remote work and gig freelancing also has broader societal implications. It can lead to a more inclusive economy, where people who might be excluded from traditional work settings due to location, health, or caregiving responsibilities can participate fully. This inclusivity can drive economic growth and social cohesion, creating a more equitable and prosperous society.

In my opinion, the transition to a remote and gig-centric work model is not just a necessity; it is an opportunity. An opportunity for businesses to become more sustainable, agile, and cost-effective. An opportunity for workers to achieve a better balance and greater job satisfaction and an opportunity for societies to foster a more inclusive and resilient economy. As we stand at the crossroads of change, the path forward is clear. Embracing the future of work is not just a smart choice; it is an imperative for a better world.

The heart of leadership in this new era pulsates with qualities like empathy, adaptability, and an unwavering commitment to the well-being of our teams. These qualities are not optional; they are the bedrock upon which the future of effective leadership rests. The journey through the pages of this book has underscored the transformative impact of a leadership style that is anchored in caring and empathy. We have seen, through numerous examples and anecdotes, how such leadership not only elevates productivity and engagement but also weaves a strong fabric of community and belonging, especially critical in remote and gig work settings.

Our journey has revealed the multifaceted challenges and opportunities that come with steering a ship into the unknown waters of the gig and remote economy. Building trust across digital platforms, creating a sense of unity in a team that might never meet face-to-face, and keeping motivation high are just a few of the hurdles that modern leaders must overcome. Yet, within these challenges lie immense opportunities: the chance to tap into a global talent pool, strike a harmonious balance between work and life, and harness the power of technology to lead more effectively.

The impending future of work demands a radical shift in the way companies operate, particularly in their approach to leadership and technology. Embracing remote and gig work is not just about adapting to new work styles; it is about fundamentally rethinking how organizations are structured and led. Companies aligned with fostering remote and gig work must invest in recruiting leaders who embody the principles of **leading with care**. This new breed of leaders understands the nuances of managing distributed teams, emphasizing empathy, communication, and trust. They are adept at nurturing a culture where remote and gig workers feel valued and integral to the company's success.

Simultaneously, investing in technology is crucial for companies preparing for this transition. Secure and compliant access to corporate tools is non-negotiable. This includes robust infrastructure supported by advanced AI monitoring and threat detection systems. Such technology ensures that remote and gig workers can work efficiently without compromising security. It is about creating a seamless, safe digital environment that replicates the security and efficiency of traditional office settings.

Companies must urgently start familiarizing themselves with gig-freelancing platforms. These platforms are more than just talent pools; they are gateways to a diverse range of skills and services that can be leveraged for various projects. Understanding how to utilize these platforms effectively will be key to tapping into the full potential of the gig economy.

To accelerate their preparation for the future of work, companies also need to focus on creating inclusive policies and support systems for remote and gig workers. This includes fair compensation, access to resources, and opportunities for growth and development. It is about building an ecosystem where remote and gig workers are seen as equal contributors to the company's objectives.

Furthermore, companies should engage in continuous learning and development initiatives to keep their workforce, both permanent and gig, up to date on the latest trends and technologies. This not only enhances the skill set of the workforce but also ensures that the company remains competitive and innovative.

Preparing for the future of work is a multifaceted endeavor and must be taken seriously by any type of organization. It requires a harmonious blend of empathetic leadership, advanced technology, strategic use of gig-freelancing platforms, inclusive policies, and a commitment to continuous learning. By focusing on these areas, companies can position themselves to thrive in the rapidly evolving landscape of work.

In an era where technology is not just a tool but a partner in our endeavors, we must recognize its potential to empower our leadership practices. From AI-driven analytics that aid in informed decision-making to digital platforms that foster collaboration and community, technology is a vital ally in our quest to lead effectively in this new era of work.

My personal reflections and learnings from this journey have been profound. I have seen firsthand the power of a leadership approach that values empathy and care and how it can transform teams and businesses. This personal journey has been a source of inspiration and a guide, underscoring the immense potential and responsibility that comes with the role of a leader.

Looking towards the horizon, the future of work and leadership appears both exciting and daunting. It is like a picture that keeps changing with new trends, challenges, and opportunities. Leaders must stay agile, embrace continuous learning, and adapt to maintain relevance and effectiveness in this dynamic landscape. This calls for a reorientation of our leadership compass to ensure that we are not only navigating correctly but are also explorers, ready to discover and adapt to the unknown terrains of work and leadership.

In concluding this journey, I offer a call to action to all current and future leaders. It is a call to embrace the principles of caring, empathetic leadership, to lead with a sense of purpose and vision, and to respect the individuality and well-being of each team member. This is not just about leading teams; it is about nurturing communities of professionals who are connected by more than just work.

In the journey of leadership, let us not forget that every step we take resonates with the rhythm of **human connection**.

As we lead through the vast, unknown areas of modern work, let our legacy be defined not just by the goals we achieve but by the hearts we touch and the lives we illuminate.

For in the end, it is the human spirit, nurtured and cherished, that truly transforms the ordinary into the extraordinary.

References

1. Owl Labs. (2019, September). State of Remote Work 2019. Retrieved from https://resources.owllabs.com/state-of-remote-work/2019.
2. Buffer. (2019). State of Remote Work 2019. Retrieved from https://buffer.com/state-of-remote-work/2019.
3. Reynolds, B. W. (n.d.). How Flexible Work Plays a Big Role in Job Choices. FlexJobs. Retrieved from https://www.flexjobs.com/blog/post/survey-flexible-work-job-choices/.
4. Benslimane, N. (2021, March 12). The Gig-Work Platforms' Market Sheds Its Skin to Face COVID's Impact. InfoMineo. Retrieved from https://infomineo.com/technology-telecommunication/the-gig-work-platforms-market-sheds-its-skin-to-face-covids-impact/.
5. Ioannou, L. (2020, September 15). A Snapshot of the $1.2 Trillion Freelance Economy in the U.S. in the Age of Covid-19. CNBC. Retrieved from https://www.cnbc.com/2020/09/15/a-snapshot-of-the-1point2-trillion-freelance-economy-in-the-us-in-2020.html.
6. PwC. (2021, January 12). US Remote Work Survey. Retrieved from https://www.pwc.com/us/en/services/consulting/business-transformation/library/covid-19-us-remote-work-survey.html.
7. Global Workplace Analytics. (n.d.). Work From Home Experience Survey Results. Retrieved from https://globalworkplaceanalytics.com/global-work-from-home-experience-survey.

8. NCH. (2022, December 26). What Will the Gig Economy Look Like in 2023? Retrieved from https://nchinc.com/blog/personal-developement/what-will-the-gig-economy-look-like-in-2023/.

9. Stiltner, M. (2023, April 14). Gig Economy Trends 2023. Rapyd. Retrieved from https://www.rapyd.net/blog/gig-economy-trends-2023/.

10. McKinsey & Company. (2023, August 2). What is the Gig Economy? Retrieved from https://www.mckinsey.com/featured-insights/mckinsey-explainers/what-is-the-gig-economy.

11. Global Workplace Analytics. (n.d.). Work From Home Experience Survey Results. Retrieved from https://globalworkplaceanalytics.com/global-work-from-home-experience-survey.

12. United States Environmental Protection Agency. (2023, May 11). Pollution from Transportation. Retrieved from https://www.epa.gov/transportation-air-pollution-and-climate-change/carbon-pollution-transportation.

13. Kacapyr, S. (2023, September 18). Lifestyle Impacts Green Benefits of Remote Work. Cornell University. Retrieved from https://news.cornell.edu/stories/2023/09/lifestyle-impacts-green-benefits-remote-work.

14. Omprakash, V. (2023, December 22). Freelance Market Statistics & Trends. Flexiple. Retrieved from https://flexiple.com/freelance/freelance-statistics-and-trends-2020.

15. TeamStage. (2023). Gig Economy Statistics: Demographics and Trends. Retrieved from https://teamstage.io/gig-economy-statistics/.

16. Gilbert, N. (2023, December 16). 405 Freelance Statistics for 2023: Market Size, Profile Data & Salary Rates. FinancesOnline. Retrieved from https://financesonline.com/freelance-statistics/.

17. Kempton, B. (2023, October 27). Gig Economy Statistics and Key Takeaways for 2023. Upwork. Retrieved from https://www.upwork.com/resources/gig-economy-statistics.

18. VitalSmarts. (2017, November 2). Virtual Reality: Remote Employees Experience More Workplace Politics Than Onsite Teammates. PR Newswire. Retrieved from https://www.prnewswire.com/news-releases/virtual-reality-remote-employees-experience-more-workplace-politics-than-onsite-teammates-300548594.html.

19. Buffer. (2020). State Of Remote Work 2020. Retrieved from https://buffer.com/state-of-remote-work/2020.

20. Hickman, A., & Maese, E. (2021, March 26). Measure Performance: Strategies for Remote and Hybrid Teams. Gallup. Retrieved from https://www.gallup.com/workplace/341894/measure-performance-strategies-remote-hybrid-teams.aspx.

21. Mueller, J., Matz, R., Damon, Z. J., Naraine, M. L., & Skinner, J. (2023, February 7). The Importance of Physical Proximity for Team Cohesion – A Case Study of USA Rugby 7s. Retrieved from https://www.tandfonline.com/doi/full/10.1080/23750472.2023.2170268.

22. Shirmohammadi, M., Au, W. C., & Beigi, M. (2022, March 10). Remote Work and Work-Life Balance: Lessons Learned from the Covid-19 Pandemic and Suggestions for HRD Practitioners. Retrieved from https://www.tandfonline.com/doi/full/10.1080/13678868.2022.2047380.

23. Lohani, M. (2022, March 1). The 6 Leadership Approaches You Need for Building Trust in Remote Teams. Knolskape. Retrieved from https://knolskape.com/blog/6-leadership-approaches-you-need-for-building-trust-in-remote-teams/.

24. Krehl, E.-H., & Büttagen, M. (2022, March). Uncovering the Complexities of Remote Leadership and the Usage of Digital Tools during the COVID-19 Pandemic: A

Qualitative Diary Study. ResearchGate. Retrieved from
https://www.researchgate.net/publication/359400572_Unco
vering_the_complexities_of_remote_leadership_and_the_u
sage_of_digital_tools_during_the_COVID-
19_pandemic_A_qualitative_diary_study.

25. Velocity Global. (2023, September 1). Adaptability in the
Workplace: How to Navigate Change at Work. Retrieved
from https://velocityglobal.com/resources/blog/adaptability-
in-the-workplace/.

26. Nink, M. (2015, October 13). Many Employees Don't
Know What's Expected of Them at Work. Gallup.
Retrieved from
https://news.gallup.com/businessjournal/186164/employees
-don-know-expected-work.aspx.

27. Perera, A. (2023, September 7). Hawthorne Effect:
Definition, How It Works, And How To Avoid It. Simply
Psychology. Retrieved from
https://www.simplypsychology.org/hawthorne-effect.html.

28. Drew, C. (PhD). (2023, May 25). Types of Communities.
Helpful Professor. Retrieved from
https://helpfulprofessor.com/types-of-communities/.

29. Psychology Today. (n.d.). Emotional Intelligence Test.
Retrieved from
https://www.psychologytoday.com/au/tests/personality/emo
tional-intelligence-test.

30. PsychTests. (n.d.). Emotional Intelligence Test. Retrieved
from https://testyourself.psychtests.com/testid/3979.

31. Alpha High IQ Society. (n.d.). What is EQ? - For Success at
Work. Retrieved from https://www.iq-test.net.

32. Human Library. (n.d.). Retrieved from
https://humanlibrary.org/